Microgreens:

A Complete Step by Step Beginners Guide for Growing Microgreens

&

Hydroponic Gardening for Beginners:

A How-To Guide for Growing Vegetables, Herbs & Fruits in Your Own Sustainable Soil-Free Home Hydroponic Garden

---

Basil Green

Download the Audio Version of 'Microgreens' FREE

This book is best enjoyed in its audio format! If you love listening to audio books on-the-go, I have great news for you. You can download the audio book version of this book for **FREE** just by signing up for a **FREE** 30-day audible trial! See below for more details!

Audible trial benefits

As an audible customer, you'll receive the below benefits with you 30-day free trial:

- Free audible copy of this book
- After the trial, you will get 1 credit each month to use on any audiobook
- Your credits automatically roll over to the next month if you don't use them
- Choose from over 400,000 titles
- Listen anywhere with the audible app across multiple devices
- Make easy, no hassle exchanges of any audiobook you don't love
- Keep your audiobooks forever, even if you cancel your membership
- And much more

Go to the links below to get started

FOR AUDIBLE US:

bit.ly/microgreensfree

FOR AUDIBLE UK:

bit.ly/microgreensfreeuk

© Copyright 2020 - All rights reserved.

The content contained within this book may not be reproduced, duplicated or transmitted without direct written permission from the author or the publisher.

Under no circumstances will any blame or legal responsibility be held against the publisher, or author, for any damages, reparation, or monetary loss due to the information contained within this book, either directly or indirectly.

Legal Notice:

This book is copyright protected. It is only for personal use. You cannot amend, distribute, sell, use, quote or paraphrase any part, or the content within this book, without the consent of the author or publisher.

Disclaimer Notice:

Please note the information contained within this document is for educational and entertainment purposes only. All effort has been executed to present accurate, up to date, reliable, complete information. No warranties of any kind are declared or implied. Readers acknowledge that the author is not engaged in the rendering of legal, financial, medical or professional advice. The content within this book has been derived from various sources. Please consult a licensed professional before attempting any techniques outlined in this book.

By reading this document, the reader agrees that under no circumstances is the author responsible for any losses, direct or indirect, that are incurred as a result of the use of the information contained within this document, including, but not limited to, errors, omissions, or inaccuracies.

Bonus!

Wouldn't it be nice to have even more motivation and inspiration on your gardening journey? As a sincere "Thank you" for reading my book, i've given you access to a FREE Indoor Gardening ebook below!

Go to This Link to Get Your Free Bonus Indoor Gardening Ebook:

bit.ly/Indoorgardeningfree

These indoor gardening tips helped me immensely with my indoor growing. I hope they help you too!

Before We Begin…

If you enjoy this book then I'd like to ask you for a favor. Would you be kind enough to

leave a review for this book on Amazon?

It'd be greatly appreciated & will likely help other avid green thumbs with their projects! I read EVERY review I receive and each one helps me to serve each and every one of you better, so your feedback is highly valued!

Thank you,

Basil Green

Table of Contents

Bonus! 5
Table of Contents 7
Introduction 12
Chapter 1 13
What Are Microgreens? 13
- The Popularity of Microgreens 13
- The Structure of Microgreens 14
- Terminology 14
- How Nutritious Are Microgreens? 14

Chapter 2 16
Tips for Growing Microgreens 16
- Is Microgreen Consumption Risky? 18
- Introducing Microgreen into Your Food 19

Chapter 3 21
Types of Microgreens 21
- Arugula 21
- Asparagus 21
- Barley 22
- Basil 22
- Beets 23
- Broccoli 23
- Buckwheat 23
- Cabbage 24
- Carrot 24
- Cauliflower 24
- Celosia 25
- Chervil 25
- Corn 25
- Endive 26

    Lettuce 26

    Mustard 26

    Radish 26

  Differences Between Microgreens and Baby Greens 27

  Popular Microgreens and Their Nutritional Value   27

Chapter 4   30

Microgreen Troubleshooting Tips 30

  Mold   30

    Troubleshooting Mold 31

  Fallen Greens   31

    Troubleshooting Fallen Greens   32

  Yellow Microgreens   32

    Troubleshooting Yellow Microgreens   33

  Clumped Greens 33

    Troubleshooting Clumped Greens 33

  Slow Germination Time 33

    Troubleshooting Slow Germination Time   33

Chapter 5   35

How to Grow Microgreens at Home   35

  Cultivating Your Microgreens   35

  Benefits of Growing Microgreens   36

Chapter 6   38

Health Benefits of Eating Microgreens   38

Chapter 7   40

Some Microgreen FAQs   40

Chapter 8   49

Some Microgreen Recipes 49

  Beef Burger   49

  Parmesan and Ricotta Cheese Pizza with Microgreens   50

  Sunflower Guacamole   52

  Mini Strawberry Chocolate Tart 52

  Sheet Pan Fajitas with Bell Peppers and Chickpeas 53

- End of Summer Salad   54
- Bacon Hash Brown Casserole with Eggs   55
- Microgreens with Strawberry-Lime Vinaigrette   57
- Lemon and Pea Tendril Risotto 58
- Mediterranean Quinoa Salad   59
- Charred Rainbow Beet and Pistachio Salad   60
- Roasted Broccoli Microgreen Soup   61
- Mushroom and Microgreen Omelet   62
- Asparagus, Tomato, and Microgreen Salad   63
- Kale and Radish Microgreen Salad   64
- Seared Sea Scallops with Microgreen Salad   65
- Seared Halibut with Microgreens Salad   66
- Microgreen, Zucchini, and Carrot Cake   67
- Super Microgreen Smoothie   68
- Blue Cheese Tomato with Microgreens 68
- Cold Smoked Salmon Sandwiches with Microgreens 69
- Vegan Microgreen Soup 70

Conclusion   72

References   73

Book 2: Hydroponic Gardening for Beginners: 74

Bonus!   75

Introduction 76

Chapter 1   77

Hydroponic Gardening: A History and Overview   77

- What Is Hydroponic Gardening?   77
- The Beginnings of Hydroponic Gardening   77
- Hydroponics for the Future   79
- Advantages of Hydroponic Gardening 80
- Disadvantages of Hydroponic Gardening   82

Chapter 2   85

Practices of Hydroponic Gardening   85

- Water Culture vs Medium Culture   85

- Water Culture 85
- Medium Culture 86
  - What Are the Hydroponic Growing Mediums? 86
- Irrigation and Feeding Techniques 90
  - Sub-Irrigation 90
  - Passive Sub-Irrigation 91
  - Top-Feeding Irrigation 91
  - Run-to-Waste 91
  - Recirculating Your Nutrient Solution 92

Chapter 3 94

Understanding Hydroponic Systems 94

- Germinating Seeds Without Soil 94
- The Six Main Hydroponic Systems 95
- Wick System 95
  - What to Grow 96
- Deep Water Culture 97
  - Variations 98
  - What to Grow 99
- Ebb and Flow 100
  - What to Grow 100
- Drip Systems 101
  - Variations 102
  - What to Grow 102
- Nutrient Film Technique 103
  - What to Grow 104
- Aeroponics 104
  - What to Grow 105
- Indoor vs Outdoor 106

Chapter 4 109

Step by Step Hydroponic Systems 109

- Wick System 109
- Deep Water Culture System 111

- Ebb and Flow System   113
- Nutrient Film Technique 115

Chapter 5   118
Hydroponic Gardening: Nutrients 118

- Macro and Micro   118
- PH Balance   118
- Not All Plants Are Equal   118
- Temperature   119
- Buy Commercial or Make Your Own 119
- Nutrient Ingredients   120
- Nutrient Deficiency   120
- Nutrient Solution: Balance and Concentration   121

Chapter 6   123
Diseases, Pests, Common Problems   123

- Common Problems   123
  - Water + Nutrients + Light = Algae   123
  - Leaks   123
  - Nutrient Deficiencies, pH, EC   124
  - Hard Water   124
  - Heat and Humidity   125
- Plant Diseases   125
  - Common Diseases   125
  - The Solution   126
- Plant Pests 126
  - Common Pests 126
  - The Solution   127

Chapter 7   128
Tips and Myths   128

- Tips for Hydroponic Gardening 128
- Hydroponic Myths Busted!   130

Conclusion   132
References   133

Introduction

Microgreens are often no bigger than 3 inches in height. They are quite young (no more than seedlings) but do not mistake that for being less nutritious. In fact, these young greens usually contain more nutrients than their more mature vegetable counterparts. And this is one reason why a lot of individuals choose them.

The aroma they bring to any dish and their rich healthy colors make for beautiful garnishes. Their high nutrient content and beautiful aesthetic might be why you've chosen to learn more about microgreens. Or perhaps you are a gardner who wishes to learn how to grow healthy microgreens. Maybe you even want to learn about both.

Whichever the case, you're reading the right book. Everything from the correct conditions for successfully cultivating microgreens to recipes made with them will be treated in this book. It also doesn't matter how much or little you know about microgreens, you're covered.

Since you're interested in microgreens, prepare yourself. This will be the most profitable and enjoyable book you've read all year. Let's get to it now.

Chapter 1

What Are Microgreens?

Microgreens is a term used to describe aromatic greens otherwise known as vegetable confetti or micro herbs, which have rich flavors and introduce a splash of color in various dishes. Regardless of their relatively small size, microgreens have rich nutritional values, making them a healthy component in any food. Microgreens typically exist as young vegetable greens with a height range of one to three inches, or 2.5 to 7.5 centimeters, including their stem and leaves. Their height range puts them in a similar class to baby greens, sprouts, and shoots, but they are a distinct category and can be classified as the stage between sprouts and baby greens. They are smaller than baby greens like radicchio, arugula, spinach, et cetera, but are harvested earlier after the sprout stage.

The distinction further widens as sprouts have a shorter growing cycle, ranging from 2 to 7 days. Microgreens, on the other hand, are typically ready for harvest between 7 to 21 days after they germinate. That is, microgreens are formed after the development of cotyledon leaves. Harvesting is done by cutting the stem just above the soil line.

The Popularity of Microgreens

Microgreens are typically purchased or grown by people with an eye for nutrition. Otherwise, they are used for their ability to lend aesthetic and flavor to food, especially by fine dining outlets. Chefs typically use microgreens for their ability to lend color while improving the taste and attractiveness of several dishes by capitalizing on their unique delicate textures and distinct flavors like spicy and sweet.

Microgreens are grown from a variety of herbs, vegetables, and other plants, and have been a regular show on the menus of chefs stretching back into the '80s in San Francisco. In the mid-90s, growing microgreens became popular in Southern California and the tradition has continued. Initially, only very few varieties of microgreens were used. Among them were kale, basil, cilantro, arugula, beets, as well as a colorful mix of those known as "Rainbow Mix." As they grew in popularity, microgreens spread to the east from California, reaching many areas in the United States where they are now grown in many varieties. In recent times, the industry for microgreens has expanded to involve several different growers and seed companies.

The Structure of Microgreens

There are three main parts common to all microgreens, namely a cotyledon leaf, a central stem, and the first pair of young true leaves. The size of microgreens differs, but the average size typically lies within the 1 to 1.5 range (2.5 to 3.8 cm). While this is the range in which a plant qualifies to be called a microgreen, some exceed this range and are regarded as petite greens. Microgreens have a life cycle of 2 to 4 weeks from seedling to harvest.

Terminology

In the true sense of the word, microgreens isn't a real word with any scientific history and is merely a construct of marketing terminology. Like "baby greens" which conceptualizes their stages of development. Conversely, the term sprouts refers to germinated seeds, which are usually eaten whole, including the shoot, seed, and roots, based on the variety.

For instance, sprouts of plants like peanuts, pumpkins, and almonds tend to have more preferable flavors when harvested earlier.

How Nutritious Are Microgreens?

In early 2014, publications from the USDA Agricultural Research Service's researchers boasted of a variety of studies that describe the nutritional value of microgreens. These studies also include vital information like their shelf life and growth cycle. According to the studies in these publications, about 25 varieties of microgreens were examined and their main nutrients measured. Among these nutrients are vitamin E (tocopherols, vitamin K (phylloquinone), vitamin C (ascorbic acid), a precursor to vitamin A (beta-carotene), among other affiliated carotenoids.

Of the 25 samples of microgreens used in the study, garnet amaranth had the highest concentration of vitamin K; red cabbage vitamin C; green daikon radish vitamin E; and cilantro carotenoids. On a general note, microgreens had higher levels of carotenoids and higher vitamin concentration (up to five times greater) than their average mature plant counterparts. This implies that microgreens may well be worth the hype and trouble of growing and delivering them fresh within their short life cycle.

In 2012, a summertime nutritional study conducted by the University of Maryland's Department of Nutrition and Food Science showed promising results implying that microgreens could contain high nutritional content in comparison to other mature veggies. At Texas A&M University, a director of the Vegetable and Fruit Improvement Center and horticulture professor, Bhimu Patil agreed on the potential of microgreens to have higher nutritional values than their mature vegetable counterparts. However, he noted that more studies would be necessary for side-by-side comparison between both varieties. While he agrees on nutrient composition, Patil is wary that discrepancies could exist in nutritional value based on factors such as the soil medium, time of harvest, and place of planting.

According to researchers from the above mentioned studies, the best and most nutritious microgreens are those that have higher color intensities. Although the nutritional value may vary across microgreens, many varieties tend to have high copper, zinc, potassium, magnesium, and iron content. Among their beneficial constituents are antioxidants which are helpful in boosting the immune system. Given their high nutrient density, microgreens have higher levels of antioxidants, minerals, and vitamins than an equal amount of their mature counterparts. However, this doesn't necessarily prove that this quality is constant across all varieties of microgreens.

Chapter 2

Tips for Growing Microgreens

1. **Proper timing is everything**: Wherever you live, whether it's cold, hot, or temperate, chances are you can cultivate some variety of microgreens some time of year outdoors or indoors. A key factor to successfully growing and harvesting microgreens is planning your time right. Planting your seed during the wrong time period will only render your resources and efforts useless. Microgreens ought to be cultivated within a short period of one to three weeks and consumed quickly for an optimal outcome.

   As such, cultivation in the right season is imperative. Some varieties require warmer climates for germination, while some may favor colder weather. Delve into planting only after carrying out your research, and pick the best time of year for your planting season. One handy lesson is to keep an age-old farming practice in mind. This logic requires growing crops in alignment with the different phases of the moon every other month.

   You will find it astonishing to know that the moon has a gravitational pull effect, which not only affects tides, but the flow of plant sap and soil moisture as well. In this light, sowing your microgreens during these periods will ensure optimal absorption of moisture and nutrients, resulting in faster growth and germination cycles.

   While seemingly trivial, this logic makes a huge difference in speeding up the cultivation of healthy "fast food" for domestic or commercial purposes. If you are worried about missing the moon's phases, you could try getting a moon calendar. They are usually sustainable, easy to use, and are applicable around the world, despite variations in climate and time zones.

2. **Protecting your plants is key**: Just like any other thing you hold dear, your plants require shelter, not only to be shielded from harsh weather conditions but from other factors as well. For microgreens grown outside, they will be exposed to other factors that might prey on them. Birds, rodents, and ants feast on seeds, so microgreens are a snack in their eyes. Hence, you need to protect your microgreen

seeds until germination. Nothing fancy, just go DIY on this tip. Try using clear lids, plastic bags, upcycled bottles, or a mini greenhouse. Doing this can help create a humid environment for proper seed germination.

3. **Prevent the formation of mold**: Mold is a killer of microgreens and should be avoided at all costs. It is particularly a problem for people living in warmer climates. The humid weather in subtopic regions aid the formation of mold, so it can quickly become a problem.

   A fan can come in handy in boosting air circulation. Most microgreens will prefer a relative humidity of 40 to 60 percent, but this can vary between plants. Also, only sowing a few seeds in a single pot or tray can help with aeration and nutrient intake, as there won't be much competition among the plants.

4. **Go easy on your microgreens:** Think of microgreens as the toddler stage in plant life, keep in mind their fragile leaves and stems which could so easily get damaged. Endeavor to treat them delicately when handling. Rather than spray with a watering can, try misting with a spray can or watering from the bottom up. Handling techniques can also vary across microgreen variety, as they exhibit different characteristics during growth. Some tend to grow short and straight, like rocket or basil, while others turn out quite tall, like buckwheat and pea shoots.

5. **Make daily observations:** Check up on your plants once or twice every other day. You might need to carry out some tasks like:

    a. Watering to improve moisture.
    b. Checking for symptoms of mold formation.
    c. Ensuring adequate air circulation and light positioning.
    d. Acting speedily to revive conditions like weakness or forward inclination.
    e. Taking off the lid, especially if you grow them in an enclosed container.
    f. Moving the plants to another space for easier access to better light for photosynthesis. This could save you the risk of leggy and spindly growth.

6. **Soil composition**: For quick, healthy, and thick growth, it is necessary to be aware of the nutrients in your seed mix. Once the seeds have germinated and spring their first true leaves, their continued healthy development rests on the moisture, light, and growing medium available to them.

   Microgreens don't require quite as much nutrition as seedlings as they don't need to grow into mature plants. Certain mixes for cultivating seeds have little to no nutrients or high sodium levels. Other growing media may tend to hold more moisture than required, thus blocking potential air pockets. Such mixes could lead to problems like damping and root rot.

While microgreens can grow and thrive in a plethora of growing media, they do vary in nutrient content and requirement over time. You can take charge of the flavor intensity, color vibrance, nutrient richness and content, and healthiness by creating your own seed growing mix. You can add trace elements and all the necessary minerals required for healthy growth. A good idea is to use liquid seaweed solutions daily or once every two days.

7. **Try repurposing seed raising mix**: While it is a bad idea to reuse the mix you used in growing your microgreens, it can come in handy when repurposed. After harvesting all your microgreens, there tends to be some leftover seeds and roots. The seeds could be as a result of not having enough room to grow and mature. If you continue to nurture the mix, you could get a second growth in due time. There's no point doing away with your seed mix now, is there?

After totally harvesting all your microgreens, the seed raising mix will be overrun with unharvested roots. Over time, it will break down and add to the organic matter content of the soil. However, without additional time and processing, trying to plant new seeds into the mix would be unwise, as there won't be room for sufficient growth and germination.

Also, you run the risk of the seed becoming contaminated by plant pathogens due to the composting process. To avoid this, try repurposing your seed raising mix by adding it to a worm farm or allowing it to compost totally. Afterward, you can use it again in your growing media for new seeds. This way, you've recycled nutrients and saved money so that you can plant more microgreens over time.

Is Microgreen Consumption Risky?

In a general sense, consuming microgreens is quite safe. However, it is noteworthy that these plants pose the risk of food poisoning. Since the probability of bacteria growth in microgreens is significantly less than in sprouts, they are a much safer alternative. Microgreens can be cultivated in environments that are less humid and warm than is necessary for sprouts, and only the stems and leaves are eaten as opposed to the seeds and roots. With that in mind, for people planning to cultivate microgreens on a small scale, getting the seeds from a reputable company is important. Also, it's important to ensure that the growing medium is devoid of contamination by harmful bacteria like *E. Coli* and *Salmonella*.

Common growing mediums for microgreens include vermiculite, perlite, and peat. Also, there are single-use growing mats specifically designed for the cultivation of microgreens. These are deemed to have high sanitary standards.

Introducing Microgreen into Your Food

This can be done in many different ways. One way is to incorporate them into a variety of dishes, such as salads, wraps, and sandwiches. Asides direct inclusion in food, they could also be juiced or blended into smoothies. For example, a common juiced form of microgreens is wheatgrass juice. Another alternative use is for garnishing dishes, such as omelets, pizzas, curries, and soups, among other warm foods.

In this light, microgreens are relatively safe. However, there are some cases in which they aren't. For instance, sprouts aren't consumed raw, due to the conditions in which they are grown (poor sunlight, ventilation, dampness, and soils). These conditions spur the growth and multiplication of fungi and bacteria, which may be harmful to health. Similarly, the soil preparation for microgreens cultivation requires lots of nutrients, which could lead to a mold growth problem.

On the other hand, microgreens do have a rather clean cultivation process, being grown in safer and cleaner conditions. However, this doesn't completely eliminate the risk of them containing harmful microbes when consumed raw. Thus, it is best to consume them after they've been rinsed off. Since the root isn't being consumed and is left out during harvesting, this also slashes the contamination potential down significantly.

But the absence of the root doesn't necessarily imply a total elimination of pathogens on microgreens. And what better way to combat microbes than good old fashion cooking, which fights off fungus, parasites, bacteria, and even spores? However, since cooking tends to reduce the nutrient integrity of microgreens, they are seldom ever cooked. The reason is that some of the enzymes and vitamins in microgreens are water-soluble. With that in mind, it's important to note the microgreens that could pose certain health risks, particularly when consumed too much.

These microgreens have a specific chemical content, which is mildly toxic to the human system. The body can handle such toxicity in small quantities, so those microgreens are entirely safe provided you follow certain instructions. Below are some of those microgreens:

1. **Quinoa**: This microgreen contains saponins, which are an anti-nutrient. However, these saponins can be easily removed during cultivation. To do this, try soaking the seeds in water, after which you run and rinse them several times to clear the soap-like suds. Quinoa seeds sold in packets tend to be pretreated to remove this quality, so you could purchase those instead.
2. **Alfalfa**: This microgreen is popular for its petite structure and is typically used raw in several soups and delicacies. However, it has a high germ content, hence there is a higher probability of infection outbreaks in its consumers. Additionally, this microgreen has a fair percentage of unhealthy compounds, including canavanine (an amino acid), and lectins and saponins, which are both anti-nutrients. While the body can handle these unhealthy compounds in small quantities, they tend to result in bloating, inflammation, indigestion, diarrhea, and symptoms similar to lupus, caused by the canavanine content, when consumed in large amounts.
3. **Buckwheat**: This is a microgreen with a fast growth cycle. It contains a compound known as fagopyrin, which can cause symptoms like swelling, redness, and burning sensations on the skin when consumed in large amounts. It makes the skin highly sensitive to sunlight, and this symptom can persist for several days. These symptoms tend to vary across people. Many reportedly haven't experienced some of these symptoms, even when consumed in bulk several times a week. Some suggest that a different variety from India could be responsible, with consuming the common local variety having a much different outcome.

Chapter 3

Types of Microgreens

Microgreens are tasty, beautiful, and nutritious. But there's more to why they are as popular as they are today: variety. With microgreens, variety is indeed the spice of life. There is no shortage of choice with microgreens. So, let's check a few of them out.

Generally, there are six popular families of microgreens.

1. Radish, cauliflower, and arugula are classified under **Brassicaceae**.
2. In the **Asteraceae** family, we have veggies like endives and lettuces.
3. Cucumbers and melons are **Cucurbitaceaes**.
4. Carrots and celery are categorized as **Apiaceaes**.
5. The **Amaranthaceae** family consists of quinoa, spinach, and beets.
6. Garlic, leeks, and onions, belongs to the **Amaryllidaceae** family.

Knowing that, let's outline some microgreens and their unique characteristics.

Arugula

Called by many names (roquette, rocket, and colewort, among others), arugula is naturally filled with antioxidants, folic acid, vitamin C, and vitamin A. This means that consuming arugula is not just good for dealing with free radicals, but also quite effective with digestion. This microgreen also contains necessary minerals such as calcium, iron, potassium,

Arugula can be grown in soil or with hydroponics. This makes it a good plant for people who like the control hydroponics offers. It has a germination period of about two days and you can harvest the plant in little over a week. The harvest period is usually no more than 8 days.

Asparagus

Otherwise known as sparrow grass, asparagus is prone to delayed germination. This does not mean that you shouldn't cultivate them. But they must be pre-soaked for at least 5 hours to wake the asparagus seeds from their dormant state.

With pre-soaking, the germination time should be around 7 days. But, you will have to wait for a minimum of 20 days to harvest the microgreens. Asparagus contains vitamin A, vitamin C, iron, magnesium, and potassium.

Barley

Barley microgreens are quite nutritious. That is, if you can get past the feeling that you're just eating grass. This grass taste is what turns many people away from consuming barley microgreens.

But, guess who doesn't mind eating grass and find barley microgreens really delicious. Livestock, dogs, and cats. They just absolutely love to munch on these greens, Rabbits can't seem to get enough of them as well. So, many times when people purchase these microgreens, they do so for their animals.

Just in case you can overlook that grassy and earthy taste, then you'd be doing your body a world of good by eating these greens.

Barley can be germinated in just 2 days, sometimes less. Their harvest time is often in little over a week. These microgreens are good for those who have diabetes and can help prevent some cancers and heart diseases. They are rich in dietary fiber, beta-carotene, vitamin E, and protein.

Basil

There are different kinds of basil microgreens and they all come with their own unique, interesting taste. Lemon Basil, Cinnamon Basil, Holy Basil, and Red Rubin Basil are just a few of them. Whether you want zesty, spicy, or sweet, basil has these varieties and more.

One downside to growing basil could be the fact that it takes a while to germinate and to become ready for harvest when planted in a cold region or climate. In the winter, harvest time can be up to two weeks. This might not seem like a long time, but two weeks isn't exactly a quick harvest in the context of microgreens. Basil microgreens can germinate in between 2-3 days.

Basil seeds are mucilaginous. This means that the seeds protect themselves from unfavorable environmental conditions by forming a gel-like capsule when they get wet. It also means that they are terribly affected by clumping. They should be spread evenly and inches apart from each other.

You can get vitamin A, C, and K, and high polyphenols from consuming basil microgreens.

Beets

This microgreen takes the most time to germinate - as much as 21 days. This means that, as a planter, you might have to wait for more than a month before harvesting your microgreen beets. When they are ready to be harvested, the beets will have a bright red stem and light green flowers. They have a taste that is similar to, but sweeter than, beetroot.

They're very easy to plant so they're great for beginners, but keep in mind that they need to be pre-soaked for about 10 hours or they won't germinate quickly enough. Most of the time, beets will germinate in 7-14 days if they are pre-soaked, and they can be harvested in 8-12 days. It is possible to grow beet microgreens in a hydroponic system but growing them in soil is generally the best method.

The taste of beets is similar to sweet chards. Although you could, of course, disagree with that. Beets are packed with potassium, calcium, protein, magnesium, zinc, and iron. They also contain vitamins A, B, C, E, and K, lutein, and beta-carotene.

Broccoli

These microgreens contain a substance called sulforaphane. It is beneficial to your health but does cause the broccoli to taste a little bitter. But not everyone reports that the broccoli microgreen is bitter. When the sulforaphane compound is not present, some say it has a mild broccoli taste.

With just a two-day germination time and a one week harvest time, it can be said that broccoli microgreens are quick to cultivate. They also contain vitamins A, C, and K. But if that isn't enough incentive to consume broccoli, they are also good preventative measures against lung and colon cancers. They also improve digestion and bone health.

Buckwheat

Hydroponics can be used to grow buckwheat. Although, it is not advised. This is because the process of growing this plant without soil is not particularly easy. Buckwheat should be kept in a humidity dome before they can safely be exposed to light. It's usually much better to just grow them traditionally. Buckwheat needs about 4 days to germinate and

7-14 days to fully mature. As a gardener, make sure to water your buckwheat once a day. Make sure it's also at the same time of the day. You want the soil to be neither dry nor soggy.

Buckwheat contains fiber, vitamin C, vitamin B, vitamin K, and folic acid.

Cabbage

Arguably, the most popular kind of cabbages are the green and red kinds. People often choose the red cabbage because it is considered the sweetest and has more vitamin C. The green cabbage contains more folate, which is a type of vitamin B that promotes the production of red and white blood cells and is needed during adolescence, pregnancy, and infancy.

Germination time for cabbage is 2-3 days, but you might have to wait 2 weeks for harvest. It's quite soft when chewed and can be really colorful on a dish - with violet stems and green tops. Cabbage provides iron, vitamin C, beta-carotene, vitamin K, and vitamin E.

Carrot

They take some time to be ready for harvest - about two weeks - but the result is a rewardingly nutritious microgreen. Using the soil method to plant carrot microgreens is considered the best way since it leads to a faster germination time.

Carrot microgreens don't have a lot to offer in terms of taste. But with nutrients like folate, calcium, sodium, and vitamin A, C, and K, they really aren't a bad addition to any meal.

Cauliflower

This crispy and flavorful vegetable is seen as one of the more easily grown microgreens. Cauliflower stems are a very light pink and purple, while the tops are a deep green. You can grow them successfully in the soil or with hydroponics. The germination time for cauliflower is between 2 to 3 days, and they can be harvested in about 2 weeks after planting.

You can get beta-carotene, iron, vitamin C, and vitamin E from eating cauliflower.

Celosia

Usually, the leaves of microgreens are green, while their stem has a different color. The case is different for celosia. Their stems are green, and they have light red leaves. They really are a pleasant sight to behold and their mild taste just completes their beauty. They have a three-day maximum germination time and can be harvested in 12 days.

As for nutritional benefits, celosia microgreens contain an abundance of calcium, phosphorus, iron, and water.

Chervil

If you love parsley, licorice, or anise, then you will enjoy chervil. While this microgreen is definitely unique, it does manage to blend these three flavors perfectly. It does this so well, in fact, that some refer to it as French parsley. They can be harvested as early as 12 days after planting, but most gardeners would wait till at least the 16th day in order to get that beautiful mix of tastes.

Germination time for chervil microgreens is in no more than 4 days, and they provide vitamins A, B, C, and D. You can also get iron, potassium, calcium, and protein from eating chervil.

Corn

The microgreen shoots of corn are usually much sweeter than mature corn. Although this depends on some factors. One is that you need to harvest the microgreens on or before the sixth day of planting. If you wait for longer, the leaves will show up, and you don't want to eat those. They contain way too much fiber and aren't exactly pleasant to eat.

The other thing you should do is make sure light does not get to the shoots. This is one reason why some gardeners might prefer hydroponics. You can grow the corn microgreens indoors and in the dark. Sunlight on the shoots causes the plant to become too fibrous and develop its leaves.

Corn microgreens can be germinated in three days max. The harvest time is between 12 and 16 days. This microgreen contains calcium, magnesium, and vitamin A, B, C, and E.

Endive

We've mentioned microgreens that are enjoyed for their tastiness. Some, like radishes, are spicy. Others are slightly sweet, like cauliflower. Endives, on the other hand, are a sharp contrast. They are mildly bitter, and it is for this particular reason that people like to cultivate them. If you are into a variety of tastes in your sandwiches, microgreen salads, and other meals, then you will enjoy endives.

On the tenth day after planting, you can usually harvest the microgreens. Depending on certain environmental factors, you might have to wait 15 days to harvest them. Typically, endives enter their adult stages on the 16th day. The germination time for endives is 3 days. Soil is the best way to grow endive baby greens. For endive microgreens, hydroponics wins.

Endives contain beta-carotene, vitamin K, folate, pantothenic acid, vitamin A, manganese, calcium, zinc, and many other vital nutrients.

Lettuce

The germination time for lettuces can take up to 4 days. They thrive under moderate heat, humidity, and constant water. This means that hydroponics is great for lettuces. The stems of lettuce are often light green. Sometimes, they are a pale white color.

The nutrients contained in your lettuce include fiber, vitamin B, vitamin K, vitamin C, and folic acid.

Mustard

Like corn, your mustard needs to do some growing in the dark. But there's a difference. The mustard seeds should spend just two days in darkness. Afterward, you can expose them to sunlight or your grow light. Under the right conditions, mustard seeds grow pretty fast. They can reach maturity in only 12 days, and this similarity is shared by most microgreens in the Brassicaceae family.

Mustard seeds are rich in vitamins A, C, E, and K, fiber, and antioxidants.

Radish

People often go for radishes because of how colorful they can be. With their red stems and vibrantly green leaves, it's little wonder that quite a number of people are taken by this microgreen. For others, their choice of radishes has little to do with its colors. They just love the spiciness. Radishes aren't so hot that they can't be enjoyed. But they still pack a kick that spice lovers keep coming back for.

Radishes take as little as a day or two to germinate. For the harvest, you need only wait 6-12 days. They can be grown in soil or hydroponically. They are deliciously crunchy and packed with vitamins A, B, C, E, and K. Your radish also contains niacin, calcium, zinc, iron, and phosphorus.

Differences Between Microgreens and Baby Greens

As stated earlier, microgreens share some similarities with baby greens. Both are harvested before they can attain maturity and contain more nutrients than fully grown veggies. For these reasons, people often confuse both greens to mean the same things. Not quite.

After seeds are planted, the next stage is sprouting. It is unlikely that you have seen this stage as it typically happens beneath the soil. Although, because of how nutrient-rich sprouts are, some folks grow them at home for consumption.

Fast forward a few days (or weeks) and you have your microgreens. At this point, the plant has now developed stems, roots, and cotyledons - the first leaves. Even though these cotyledons are not mature leaves, they can still perform the function of photosynthesis.

If you allow the microgreens to grow some more, you will have the baby greens. These plants are not fully matured, but they have outgrown cotyledons for true leaves. Usually, plants are more nutritious the less mature they are. This means that sprouts are richer than microgreens. And microgreens have more nutrients than baby greens.

Popular Microgreens and Their Nutritional Value

The serving size for these microgreens is 100 g, and the nutritional value is for raw greens.

Arugula

Calories: 25 Total Fat: 0.7 g Sodium: 27 mg Total Carbs: 3.7 g Protein: 2.6 g Potassium: 369 mg Cholesterol: 0 mg

Beets

Calories: 43 Total Fat: 0.2 g Sodium: 78 mg Total Carbs: 9.6 g Protein: 1.6 g Potassium: 325 mg Iron: 0.80 mg

Buckwheat

Calories: 343 Total Fat: 3.4 g Sodium: 1 mg Total Carbs: 72 g Protein: 13 g Potassium: 460 mg Iron: 2.20 mg

Cabbage

Calories: 25 Total Fat: 0.1 g Sodium: 18 mg Total Carbs: 6 g Protein: 1.3 g Potassium: 170 mg Iron: 0.47 mg

Cauliflower

Calories: 25 Total Fat: 0.3 g Sodium: 30 mg Total Carbs: 5 g Protein: 1.9 g Potassium: 299 mg Cholesterol: 0 mg

Corn

Calories: 86 Total Fat: 1.2 g Sodium: 15 mg Total Carbs: 19 g Protein: 3.2 g Potassium: 270 mg Iron: 0.52 mg

Endives

Calories: 17 Total Fat: 0.2 g Sodium: 22 mg Total Carbs: 3.4 g Protein: 1.3 g Potassium: 314 mg Iron: 0.83 mg

Lettuce

Calories: 15 Total Fat: 0.2 g Sodium: 28 mg Total Carbs: 2.9 g Protein: 1.4 g Potassium: 194 mg Cholesterol: 0 mg

Mustard

Calories: 27 Total Fat: 0.4 g Sodium: 20 mg Total Carbs: 4.7 g Protein: 2.9 g Potassium: 384 mg Iron: 1.64 mg

Radish

Calories: 16 Total Fat: 0.1 g Sodium: 39 mg Total Carbs: 3.4 g Protein: 0.7 g Potassium: 233 mg Cholesterol: 0 mg

Chapter 4

Microgreen Troubleshooting Tips

As excited as you might be to begin cultivating your own microgreens, you must understand that the process isn't always entirely smooth. Even with the simplest of methods, things could still go wrong. Sometimes, awfully so. And the proper thing to do is prepare yourself for such eventualities.

Now you're probably wondering which eventualities, right? Here they are.

Mold

For most beginner growers, there will be no escaping this problem. Those who use hydroponics are more prone to this issue. A few things could give rise to mold or mildew as you grow your microgreens. It could be that your plant's environment is too soggy. While greens need sufficient amounts of moisture to grow well, it's also important that there isn't too much water.

High levels of humidity, poor ventilation, and inadequate supply of direct light are also contributing factors to the growth of mold and mildew.

In some cases, the problem really isn't mold or anything similar. Sometimes, those who aren't experienced in gardening might confuse the structure of root hairs for mildew.

To differentiate the two (root hair and mildew), just keep these tips in mind.

1. Root hair is only found on the roots, and mildew can be found even between the microgreens.
2. Root hair appears fuzzy, while mildew seems more like a spider's web.
3. If you rinse the roots, the root hairs will disappear for hours. Mildew will remain visible even after rinsing.
4. Mildew has a slimy feel, while root hairs do n0t.
5. Root hair has no smell to it, but mildew is quite musty.

Troubleshooting Mold

1. Sometimes, the environment is perfect and it is the seedlings themselves that demand your attention. Seeds are not healthy by default and shouldn't be planted without proper sanitization. This is where pre-soaking comes into play. The time needed for pre-soaking is not the same for every seed, and the temperature of the water also differs. Generally, you can let seeds sit in a bowl of water containing one teaspoon of hydrogen peroxide for about 3 hours.

   This not only reduces the chances of mold growth but the germination time as well. You can expect a quicker harvest than if you hadn't pre-soaked the seeds.

2. Gardeners often go a step further and choose hybrid seeds that are able to resist mold growth. Your chances of getting a good buy, of course, depends on the company you're purchasing from. As such, you want to only buy seeds from trusted brands. The seeds are to be of the highest quality.

3. If there are too many people in a room with limited air supply, a single toilet, as much food as they need, and no way to get out - you can tell how that situation would go, first a messy problem, then tragic. The same goes for crops that are suffering from overseeding. As they sprout, become seedlings, and then microgreens, it will become increasingly difficult to get air to reach the individual plants.

   And this is just right for mold formation. With the area in mind, it is important to keep a few inches between the seeds. The less dense your seedlings are, the less likely you'll have to deal with mold.

4. Since the most common cause of mold formation is an overly wet environment, you have to find a solution for this. The design for most hydroponic systems already comes with a good way to handle this problem: drainage. It has to allow for proper soil aeration and prevent erosion.

Fallen Greens

One of the hardest things to watch is a microgreen leaning over and slowly, but certainly, wilting. Without question, it hurts to watch something you've put quite a bit of effort into turn brown and lifeless.

There are a number of reasons for microgreens to keel over in this way. Too little water supply, poor environmental factors (temperature, light, humidity, nutrients, pH, etc.), and overseeding are just a few of them.

But there are ways to prevent this from happening. And even if the microgreens lie seemingly lifeless, there are ways to revive them.

Troubleshooting Fallen Greens

1. You will find that water - whether in excess or otherwise - is the cause of many of the problems that affect microgreens. And when it comes to plants falling over, water is often the problem and solution.

   Try adding some water to your microgreens, and they will most likely bounce back. Remember that microgreens need water in varying amounts. Radishes, for instance, need a lot of water to grow healthy, while quinoa needs far less.

   So, to fix the problem, you shouldn't just water the microgreens. You need to learn how much that particular green needs and provide it.

2. Upon planting your seeds, the expectation is that they will grow as tall as they need to. But there is such a thing as too tall. When this happens, the stem becomes too thin and weak. Eventually, the plants succumb to gravity and fall.

   This (microgreens getting too tall) is usually the result of leaving the plants in the dark for longer than necessary. They will continue growing upward and eventually the stems will no longer be thick enough to support them. The longer the microgreens stay in darkness, the thinner they will be.

   The simple solution here is to expose the plants to sunlight when it's due.

Yellow Microgreens

If you are new to planting microgreens, this could seem like a serious problem and might even cause some panic. While it's unusual, it doesn't mean the end of your crops. This issue is caused by not taking off the blackout dome soon enough. Since they haven't been exposed to sunlight, the seedlings will turn yellow.

Troubleshooting Yellow Microgreens

1. All you need to do is remove the blackout dome. For most greens, it's even better if you take it off early. Afterward, make sure the plants get adequate sunlight.

Clumped Greens

This happens for the same reason as the mold problem: planting too many seeds in the same area. Gardeners, even experienced ones, plant large numbers of seeds because they want a higher yield. Often, this ends up being counterproductive.

There are always a finite number of resources that different plants can struggle for. With the issue of clumps, the resource is the area of land you are cultivating. Since there isn't enough space between each seed, the microgreens will push against each other as they grow. Some plants may be lifted out of the soil with their roots exposed.

Troubleshooting Clumped Greens

1. The first and most obvious solution is to allow for more space between each seed. This also means decreasing the number of seeds you plant in a single area. You have a better chance of getting higher yields if you plant fewer seeds.
2. The second tip is to make sure that your seeds are spread evenly on the tray. This can be a little difficult at first, but it will eliminate the problem of clumps.

Slow Germination Time

As we've learned from chapter three, microgreens typically grow really fast. Most, taking no more than 4 days. But this isn't always the case. You might notice if you try to cultivate a microgreen, that it takes longer than it should to germinate. If you are certain that the seed has gone past its normal germination time, there are a few things you can do.

Troubleshooting Slow Germination Time

1. The first thing you should make sure of is that the seeds are of the best quality. Before you plant them, perform a germination test by covering the seeds with a wet paper towel.

2. You could also try to enhance the germination of your plants by placing a heavy object on them. The item should be weighted, but not so heavy that it completely crushes them.
3. Finally, there is pre-soaking. This is a good way to "wake" the seeds up. Different seeds require varying pre-soak times. Some need just 4 hours, while others might require up to 12 hours of pre-soaking.

Chapter 5

How to Grow Microgreens at Home

So, you've decided to cultivate microgreens. That's great. You should understand that nothing is ever entirely an easy process. But the process of growing microgreens is not just fun, it is also quite rewarding. Let's get right to it.

When it comes to microgreens, there are a host of plants to grow. From buckwheat to beets and lettuces. Just take your pick.

Some of the things you will need to start growing these vegetables are;

1. Grow light. Alternatively, you can find a window in the south-side of your chosen room that also has good access to sunlight.
2. A shallow container where you will add you grow media and seeds.
3. A warming mat. This isn't a compulsory tool, but it does help to hasten germination.
4. Your preferred microgreen seeds.
5. Growing media and organic soil.

Cultivating Your Microgreens

1. The first thing you want to do is find that part of the room where adequate sunlight can get to your plants. If you would rather use a grow light, that's fine. They aren't expensive either. The grow lights allow for more mobility and flexibility. You can plant your microgreens anywhere you feel is more comfortable and even at times of the year when there isn't much sunlight.
2. It's time to do some clearing. If you will be planting outdoors, clear a small area of land. For indoor planting, add the organic soil to the bottom of your tray. It should rise only an inch up from the bottom of the tray. Even the soil out.
3. Now, you can spread the seeds on the soil. Make sure the seeds are even. Pre-soak the seeds the night before to speed up the time it will take the seeds to sprout.

4. Again, add soil to your tray. This soil is to cover the seeds, and this should also be even. Spray clean water on the soil. Contaminated water can lead to serious problems later on, so make sure the water has been filtered.
5. Next, you can keep the container in the part of the room that receives the most sunlight. Alternatively, place it under your grow light.
6. For a few days afterward, continue spraying the clean, filtered water onto the soil. Sogginess is a problem, but so is dryness.
7. In about 4 days, the seeds should have germinated and microgreens should appear before 4 weeks. Harvest them.
8. You can cut off the roots of the microgreens and replant them. You could also replace everything in the container. The choice is entirely yours.

Benefits of Growing Microgreens

1. Depending on the variety of plants you are cultivating, microgreens grow quite fast. Whether you want to sell them or are just growing them for personal consumption, you can harvest your microgreens in 3 weeks or less.
2. You want a quick yield. You want a high yield. But, something you probably don't know you want yet is a high yield/space ratio. Even though you should not attempt to grow too many seeds in a small area, you *can* grow an impressive amount in a small space.
3. You will need to spend a relatively small amount of time, effort, and money to cultivate any microgreen of your choice. In only a short while, you can cultivate your "fast food". The amount of money, time, or effort you will have to spend will depend mostly on the system of cultivation you use. For example, soil-less or hydroponic methods are often more expensive to set up.
4. As a result of how little space is needed to cultivate microgreens, they are a good fit for people who don't have enough room to do any planting. If you are also very busy, then you want to cultivate plants that won't require too much maintenance and grow quickly: microgreens.
5. There are only a few things needed to cultivate microgreens. If you have your growing medium, a shallow container (tray) for planting, the seeds, good lighting, and water, then you're good to go. Depending on the technique of cultivation you choose, you might need more or fewer things. But, generally, microgreens don't need much. This means you'll save money by planting microgreens.

6. Microgreens have been known to thrive regardless of climate. The season doesn't matter as much as you think it would. Hot or cold; rainy or arid; microgreens have a great chance at survival. This is not to mean that you can abandon the plants to fend entirely for themselves. But if you play your part by pre-soaking seeds, providing water, managing the environment, etc., then you have a high probability of getting a good yield regardless of the time of year you're planting.
7. And we can't complete this list without considering the fact that microgreens are typically nutrient-dense foods. They are packed with so many nutrients and are so healthy that there is another list in this book outlining the health benefits of microgreens. Check the next chapter.

Microgreens are a tasty, aesthetically satisfying, nutritious, and incredibly palatable food choice.

Chapter 6

Health Benefits of Eating Microgreens

Everyone from your doctor to your grandma knows that eating veggies is linked to a reduced susceptibility to developing certain diseases. And since microgreens are, well, greens, you know that they are one of the healthiest things to consume. These benefits stem from the high volume of plant compounds, minerals, and vitamins they contain. Below are some benefits of eating microgreens.

1. **It reduces the risk of heart problems**: Microgreens have a high polyphenol content, a category of antioxidants related to decreasing the risk of developing heart problems. Studies of this quality in animals revealed that microgreens may, in fact, reduce poor LDL cholesterol levels and decrease triglycerides in the body. A study carried out on rats fed a diet with high fat content that was supplemented with red cabbage microgreens showed a decline in weight gain by up to 17%. Furthermore, triglycerides were down by 23%, while bad LDL cholesterol decreased by 34% (Huang, 2016).
2. **It lowers the chance of chronic ailments:** Vegetables have been shown to have great health benefits, as a result of their nutrient value and polyphenol levels. Thus, vegetable consumption has been linked to the reduction of specific types of chronic ailments. Vegetable intake decreases the risk of inflammation, as well as lowering the risk of obesity. Since microgreens have a very similar nutritional and polyphenol content, more even in comparison to mature plants, they likely also have many benefits in tackling these ailments.
3. **It helps prevent Alzheimer's disease:** Due to their high antioxidant content and richness in polyphenols, microgreens could prove handy in decreasing susceptibility to Alzheimer's disease.
4. **It prevents diabetes**: Since stress can inhibit proper sugar absorption on a cellular level, antioxidants can be helpful in combating this stress. Laboratory studies on fenugreek microgreens showed an improvement in the ability of cells to absorb sugar by as much as 25 to 44 percent. Microgreens are typically found to have an effect on type 2 diabetes.
5. **Microgreens are convenient and easy to use:** For people who haven't really turned to regular consumption of vegetables and fruits, microgreens can come in

handy in helping get started. Lots of people enjoy growing microgreens as they are easier, faster, and more convenient to cultivate. As a matter of fact, one need not have a full-scale garden or a backyard to cultivate or raise microgreens. Provided one has a bit of water, the seeds, soil, and a source of light (window), that is enough to start a mini garden of microgreens. Most importantly, microgreens come in handy for new and impatient gardeners.

The wait time for cultivating microgreens is minimal as these plants can be grown, harvested, and ready for use within 7 to 14 days past germination.

6. **It can help fight certain cancers:** The antioxidant content in vegetables and fruits, particularly those with equally high polyphenol content, can help decrease one's susceptibility to certain types of cancer. Although not all forms of cancer are easily combated, those typically affected by vegetables include cancers of the digestive tract and prostate cancer. Microgreens with high levels of polyphenol may have similar qualities.

Chapter 7

Some Microgreen FAQs

1. What are microgreens?

They are younger plants, usually vegetables, that are harvested at about 1-3 weeks after planting. This is just after they produce their cotyledons or first leaves. However, not every microgreen can be eaten at the same stage, as some must be allowed to mature further and others need to be harvested early. Microgreens are becoming more popular because they provide dishes with a wide range of flavor, look, texture, and nutritional benefits.

2. Are there risks in eating microgreens?

Microgreens are often consumed raw, and this means that it is necessary to care for them diligently when they are still growing. First, since they may be grown in humid conditions and in close proximity to each other, water can be trapped leading to decay and mildew growth. Be sure to space your seeds far enough apart and ensure adequate ventilation to prevent this. Also, ensure that your plants are not exposed to infectious organisms like bacteria or fungi from other plants. Finally, ensure you buy your seeds from a reputable source such as a supermarket chain or well-known farm that performs regular and strict food safety checks.

Also, consider the water source. Do not use water that may be contaminated, like spring water or rain water that has not been treated. Planting microgreens outdoors may expose them to worms and insects. Also, check properly to ensure the microgreens you're buying are not moldy or rotten and that it has not been eaten by insects.

3. How can microgreens be grown at home?

With hydroponics, you can grow microgreens without the need for fertilizer and soil. The basics are just water, a nutrient mix, and light and it can be done commercially. You can easily grow microgreens in your home. Be careful while handling them because they are fragile young plants. Don't forget to make sure the seeds have enough room for growth and germination.

They appear small but that doesn't take away their need for adequate air circulation. The microgreens will decay if their surroundings are too stuffy or humid. Don't place them directly under the sunlight. A suitable temperature range for them is 77-90°F (25 - 32°C).

4. What is the best way to care for microgreens?

You can care for microgreens if you grow them in coconut coir water or thin mat water. A low maintenance method would be by placing the greens on a cookie tray. Cover with a lid and pour in a cup of water every day. Another option is to let them remain in their containers and open the lid so that condensation will not occur. If condensation occurs, the greens wither and die. If you will be away for some time, place them in a cool room with a temperature of less than 75°F (24°C) and good ventilation or in the fridge. They will be viable for 7-10 days without regular care with this method.

5. Which microgreens are the easiest to grow?

The brassica family is known for being easy to grow. Members of this family include cauliflower, broccoli, cabbages, etc. Another easy microgreen is anything in the mustard family. Chia is known as one of the easiest microgreens. Growers who use a hydroponic microgreens kit are provided with the easiest seeds, this is especially helpful if they are just starting. But for those planting in soil, the easiest microgreens are buckwheat and sunflower.

6. Which microgreens are most difficult to grow?

Some of the more difficult microgreens include beets, amaranth, and arugula. Some also find it tough to grow chard and chives. However, stepping up to the challenge of growing these tough microgreens is the reason why it's an interesting pastime.

7. Can microgreens grow back after cutting? (How is it done?)

No. Regrowth is not common.

However, the microgreen still has a good survival rate if it has a minimum of one healthy leaf remaining. This is due to the fact that photosynthesis will be ongoing in the presence of light. But there will be a slower growth rate and this will eventually cause stunted growth.

Also, microgreens that are obtained from second harvests do not taste exactly the same as those from the first harvest

But there are some with better chances of regrowth like snow peas, speckled peas, field peas, green peas, and fava beans. Although the rate of regrowth for most other microgreens can be described as negligible. There is also a chance that what you see as regrown microgreens may just be late sprouted seeds.

Well, this just goes to show that trying for a second harvest may not be a good idea. Rather than dwelling on that, you can turn the remains from your harvest into compost.

8. Which seeds should be pre-soaked?

You should pre-soak sunflower, pea, and buckwheat seeds for 6 to 8 hours in cold water before planting them. Beet seeds should be pre-soaked, also in cold water, for a duration of one to two hours. In addition, broccoli, kale, chard, and radish seeds would benefit from pre-soaking. Note that seeds which become coated with a gel-like substance after contacting moisture may be difficult to spread after pre-soaking, so many choose not to soak them. These include basil, mustard, flax, and chia.

9. Why is it necessary to cover the microgreens so that they're in the dark for some time?

One important requirement for growing a microgreen into a long and superfine seedling is to cover it in the dark.

When it gets dark, the microgreens seek a light source by stretching out. The result is a longer, thinner and very tender microgreen. This may look good but there is only a small amount of starch in the endosperm, and eventually, the microgreens will use up all the energy and fall over. This is the reason for pegging the blackout phase at about 1-3 days after germination for a period of 3-5 days.

Photosynthesis will start as soon as you expose them to light, and the microgreens will become sturdy and thicker. Don't forget, however, that some microgreens are naturally short and will not increase much in height.

10. When is the right time to let microgreens receive light?

As stated above, most microgreens should be exposed to light only after blocking the light out for 3-5 days. The microgreens will start to look yellowish and pale. However, this duration is not suitable for all microgreens. You have to consider some factors. For instance, there are some microgreens that grow slowly like oregano or thyme, and they require stretching for longer periods in the dark. The ideal duration for this group is 5-8 days. But the fast growers like kale and broccoli can do just fine with 2-3 days of darkness.

Another thing to consider is the environment, cultivars, and seed quality.

You need to be very alert because the microgreens do not hesitate to turn green soon after they are exposed to light. The shoot thickens according to the increase in the production of glucose. When they are at this stage, you need to increase the water supply and prevent mold infestation by creating an effective air ventilation system.

11. When should microgreens be watered?

Large clusters of microgreens are often grown in a small area, and one factor that determines their survival is the water capacity. In fact, it is a lack of water that often makes the microgreens fall over. The normal process is to maintain the moisture by watering the microgreens' tray twice daily.

Consider the soil mixture and the local weather pattern (temperature and humidity) before you water.

Basically, good soil is one that allows water to drain out quickly so the environment is not soggy but also leaves the microgreen with enough water.

You can lighten your soil by adding 20% perlite. That way, the root has access to more air which boosts its water retention capacity.

Do an inspection on the upper and lower soil to check that it is not soggy but wet enough. The bottom watering option is better for small and feathery microgreens. When you use it, simply top up water to it every other day. Don't forget to raise the tray up before you check.

There are microgreens that naturally require more water, like the dun pea and the sunflower, and there are those that don't like the broccoli and cress. But generally, microgreens need more water as they grow bigger.

12. At what point do I use soil vs. hydroponics?

Microgreens can always be grown in soil. It may be difficult to cultivate some crops using hydroponics like pea, sunflower, beet, buckwheat, cilantro, etc. For these, you will likely have more success with a soil-based growing method, kits for this are available commercially. For other microgreens, you can definitely try a hydroponic system if you prefer.

13. Are growing lights very important?

Growing lights can be useful when it comes to exposing your microgreens to light at the right time and in the right amount. However, they are not required as you can expose microgreens to fluorescent light, direct sunlight, or incandescent light instead. Grow lights, especially LED grow lights, are preferable because they are lightweight, do not use much energy, and emit very little heat. Not only that, but they also provide the plants with the blue and red parts of the spectrum that they need. Further, the grow light setup can be adjusted and timed exactly as the microgreens require.

14. What makes LED grow lights the wise choice for microgreens?

LED lights are superior because they don't emit heat and use less electricity when compared with normal grow lights. Other grow lights release white light which doesn't have the optimal spectrum for growing plants, examples of this type of light include fluorescent light and T-5 bulbs. Plants absorb the blue and red ends of the light spectrum in order to perform photosynthesis, and LED grow lights are created to provide plants with the exact light spectrum they need. LEDs are even better than sunlight in terms of making microgreens greener and healthier.

15. Why are some parts of my crops rotten?

There are a lot of things that can cause rot. The major reason is that water is very alkaline. To adjust your water to a suitable pH, use a pH balancing kit. Another reason could be that the seeds are being overwatered or they were planted too thickly.

16. Why are my crops wilting?

Crops wilt when they are not watered enough or they are exposed to excess heat.

17. Do I need to stabilize the pH of my water?

Balancing the pH of the water used in growing is highly important. Although most growers don't believe that pH matters, it does.

18. Why are my crops pale?

The crops are pale because they may not be absorbing enough light. Grow them outdoors or place them by a window to access sunlight. They may tilt towards the light so rotate frequently. Another better option is to use LED grow lights.

19. Why are there burned or dry sections on the leaves of my crops?

The reason for this is because the plants are either getting excess light or the light is coming too early.

20. What action should I take if I perceive a musty odor?

If you're using a hydroponic system, the odor usually occurs if the grow pad has been used for longer than 10 days. There is usually no odor before 10 days. However, you shouldn't see this as a problem, especially as the normal harvest time for most crops is 10 days. However, if you're using a soil-based system, the musty smell may be originating from excess moisture trapped in between microgreen stems. In this case, it is important to remove the moisture or the problem may escalate to rot or mold.

21. Why are my crops growing slowly?

The crops may be growing slowly because they are too cold. This could be especially prevalent if your trays are placed on granite countertops or tile. If you have to put them on countertops, use a towel as an insulator. If this doesn't solve your issue, consider obtaining a heating pad and placing it under your tray. If you're growing your microgreens outside, consider investing in a greenhouse.

22. What can I do to preserve my remaining microgreens if I need to go on a trip and would not be able to care for it?

Find an airtight container and line the bottom with a paper towel. Cut your leftover microgreens and put them into the container. Put another layer of paper towel on it. Place the container if cut microgreens in the refrigerator or carry them along with you. If you are carrying them along, use a cooler and ice pack to preserve it.

23. Are all microgreen growing mats or pads compostable?

Whether a growing mat or pad can be composted depends on whether it is biodegradable. For example, the hydroponic system Sure-to-Grow pads are not made from natural fiber so they cannot be composted, although some claim that they outperform other options. If you're interested in sustainable hydroponic growing, consider choosing an alternate mat such as a Micro Mat grow pad, which is made from wood fibers and can be composted. In the case of soil-based systems, you can compost the spent soil mat that the root structure of your crop holds together.

24. How can I differentiate between sprouts, microgreens, and baby salad greens?

They are different because they are various growth stages of a plant.

The sprouts represent the beginning of seed development and do not need a growing medium (soil). Instead, when they sprout, they are raised in a sprouting bag, jar or tray and then rinsed. They become edible immediately after the seeds germinate and are quite crunchy.

Microgreens are cultivated in a growing medium or soil. They mark the second stage of a plant's development. They become rooted and produce their first leaves (cotyledons), and at this point, they can be harvested before they begin to produce their true leaves. When plants are in the microgreens stage, they are tastier and have been able to soak in micronutrients and trace elements from the growth medium (soil).

Baby salad greens are attained by allowing the plant to grow for 1-2 weeks after the microgreen stage. At this stage, the true leaves have developed and the greens are harvested as young plants. The taste is a little closer to what it will be when they are adult plants.

25. How nutritious are microgreens?

Even though microgreens are harvested at a much earlier stage of growth than vegetables, their nutritional content is high. Research reports from the United States Department of Agriculture and other scientific journals state that microgreens have more nutritional value than adult vegetables. For instance, a regular gram of broccoli has two to three times less nutritional content than broccoli microgreens. Microgreens are known for their antioxidant properties.

26. Do microgreens taste different than their vegetable counterparts?

Because microgreens are eaten at a young stage, they have a more delicate and, arguably, enhanced taste when compared to adult vegetables. This delicate taste is why they are typically eaten raw and make great additions to salads or side dishes. However, their taste is determined by the species of vegetable and the farming method used. Thus, they will taste similar to their mature vegetable counterparts.

27. What varieties of microgreens are most common?

In theory, every vegetable has a microgreen which is the younger stage of its growth. But some microgreen species are more prominent because of their growth conditions, appearance, and taste. Some of the most famous ones include celery, lettuce, red cabbage, basil, kale, and spinach. Some less popular microgreens are buckwheat, radish, and mustard greens.

28. How long is the shelf life of microgreens?

The best time to eat microgreens is when they're fresh. This means buying them only when you're ready to eat them. If you can't get your microgreens the same day you want to eat them, then they can remain fresh if you keep them in the fridge, but first, wrap them in a damp paper towel. The handling conditions of the microgreens you're using differs according to the kind of plant the adult vegetable is. Don't use them in your dish until you have all the necessary information from the producer.

29. What is the best way to prepare microgreens?

Microgreens are delicate. As such, they are better used when served fresh. A lot of chefs use them as toppings for a fresh garden salad or to brighten up the color of another prepared dish or add zest to it. Only under very rare circumstances are they cooked. If the dish you have to prepare needs the microgreens to be heated, then don't forget that bad preparation can cause the microgreens to wilt quickly or burn. The best method of cooking is to saute it.

Sauteeing involves exposing the microgreens to very high heat for only a little time. It is simple to carry out. Just heat a little quantity of oil or butter in a pan. Don't use too much oil so that the microgreens do not drown inside. When the pan is hot enough, put in the microgreens and allow them to cook for just enough time to scorch the outside. This process traps the flavor and moisture in and keeps it from being soggy.

30. What types of meals can I add microgreens to?

Raw preparation is the best for microgreens. You can add them to your Burgers, Sandwiches, Salads, Tostadas, Tacos, Smoothies, Hotdogs, Wraps. Better still, just get different varieties and make a microgreen salad. You can eat your microgreens with everything.

31. How many microgreens should I eat?

Like all foods, you can eat as many as is healthy. Since microgreens are usually low in calories, you can eat quite a lot indeed.

32. Can pregnant women consume microgreens?

Generally, microgreens are safe for pregnant women. These women, however, are advised to not consume raw sprouts. This is because bacteria such as *E. coli* and *Salmonella* can easily get into the seeds and can result in premature birth or miscarriage. If the sprouts are well cooked (stir fried, for example), then it's alright for pregnant women to eat them. Sprouts differ from many microgreens in that their roots can be eaten.

33. What makes microgreens so expensive?

A large amount of labor is required to grow microgreens and this is why they are much more expensive than the adult leafy greens.

34. If I purchase microgreens, how can I wash them?

Microgreens are often delivered raw and unwashed to keep them fresh. Since they're raw, they should be washed. Simply rinse them under running water and pat them dry with a clean cloth or paper towel. Alternately, you can dry them in a salad spinner.

35. How can I store my microgreens properly before use?

Keep the microgreens in a closed container at a temperature of 38-40°F (3-5°C) preferably in a fridge. Some, like Basil, are sensitive to low temperatures and if kept in a temperature below 32°F (0°C) will change appearance to black or dark brown after a few hours.

Chapter 8

Some Microgreen Recipes

Beef Burger

Prep Time: 15 minutes

Cook Time: 10 minutes

Total Time: 25 minutes

Servings: 6

Ingredients

To make the burger:

- ½ cup microgreens of choice
- 2 lb ground beef, grass-fed
- ½ cup feta cheese, crumbled
- 1 tbsp olive oil
- 1 ½ tbsp chipotle-adobo sauce
- 6 brioche buns
- 1 tbsp butter
- Freshly ground black pepper
- 1 ½ tsp kosher salt

To make the aioli:

- ¼ tsp ground mustard
- 2 large garlic cloves
- 2 tbsp fresh lemon juice
- 1 tsp kosher salt
- ¼ cups olive oil
- 1 cup fresh mint leaves, loosely packed
- 1 ripe avocado

To make the pickled onions:

- 1 minced red onion
- ½ cups apple cider vinegar
- 1 ½ tsp kosher salt
- 1 tbsp sugar

Directions

1. Put 1 cup of water, vinegar, 1 tbsp of sugar, and 1 ½ tsp of salt in a bowl and combine. After the salt and sugar have dissolved, pour the mixture into a jar containing the red onions. Set aside at room temp. for 1 hour.
2. Get an immersion blender and add your garlic cloves, mustard, 1 tsp salt, lemon juice, ¼ cups of olive oil, mint, and avocado to its base. Set to high speed, and process until you have a smooth mix. Alternatively, you could use a food processor.
3. Now, mold the ground beef into 6 patties. They should all be 1 inch thick. Press down with your thumb to make an indentation at the center of the patties. Next, put the burgers in your fridge.
4. Heat your oven up to 350 degrees F.
5. Drizzle some of the chipotle-adobo sauce on your brioche buns. Bake them in your oven for 6 minutes.
6. Melt olive oil and butter in a large skillet placed over high heat. Take the patties from the fridge and brown them in the pan. If you want the patties medium rare, then 6 minutes of cooking should suffice.
7. After cooking all the patties, set them aside to cool.
8. Arrange the burgers in this way: bun, aioli, patty, onions, feta cheese, microgreens, and close with another bun.

Nutritional Information

Calories: 564 Total fat: 33 g Total carbs: 8.2 g Protein: 55.6 g

Parmesan and Ricotta Cheese Pizza with Microgreens

Prep Time: 1 hour

Cook Time: 18 minutes

Total Time: 1 hour 18 minutes

Servings: 4-8

Ingredients

To make the dough:

- 3 tbsp organic olive oil
- ¾ cup boiled water
- 1 tsp sea salt
- 2 ½ tsp dry active yeast
- 1 tbsp local honey
- 2 cups organic whole wheat flour

To make the toppings:

- ½ cup microgreens
- ½ cup ricotta cheese
- 4 diced smoked bacon
- ½ cup shredded parmesan cheese
- ¼ cup minced pistachios
- 2 tbsp olive oil
- ¼ tsp sea salt
- ½ tsp freshly ground pepper

Directions

1. Put yeast, water, and honey in a bowl. Combine for about 5 minutes to make the mixture frothy.
2. Next, add oil and mix some more.
3. Get a second bowl and mix salt and flour. Pour this mixture in the first bowl and, using a wooden spoon, mix some more. Set the bowl aside for the dough to swell.
4. After sitting for 45 minutes, beat the dough down and cover the bowl with a plastic wrap. Put this bowl in your refrigerator.
5. Preheat your oven to 500 degrees F.
6. Spread the dough in a pizza baking pan and sprinkle with cornmeal.
7. Get a bowl and add pepper, ricotta, salt, parmesan, and olive oil. After mixing, pour the ingredients on the pizza dough. Add diced bacon and ½ of the pistachios.
8. Put the pizza in the oven and bake for 18 minutes. You want the bacon to be brown and crispy.

9. Garnish with microgreens and ½ of the pistachios.

Nutritional Information

Calories: 229 Total fat: 10.7 g Total carbs: 27.5 g Protein: 6.1 g

Sunflower Guacamole

Prep Time: 5 minutes

Cook Time: 0 minutes

Total Time: 5 minutes

Servings: 4

Ingredients

- ½ minced jalapeno
- 2 avocados
- ¼ cup minced red onion
- ½ cup lime juice
- ⅔ cup chopped sunflower shoots
- ¼ tsp salt

Directions

1. First, add salt, avocado, and lime juice into a bowl. Mix well and add minced red onion, sunflower shoots, and jalapeno.

Nutritional Information

Calories: 191 Total fat: 15 g Total carbs: 15 g Protein: 4 g

Mini Strawberry Chocolate Tart

Prep Time: 5 minutes

Cook Time: 15 minutes

Total Time: 20 minutes

Servings: 2

Ingredients

To make the filling:

- 1.5 oz goat cheese
- 1 ½ cups strawberries
- ½ cup basil microgreens
- 1 tbsp maple syrup
- 2 tbsp Greek yogurt

To make the crust:

- ¼ cup coconut oil
- 1 cup almond flour
- 2 tbsp maple syrup
- ½ tsp salt
- 1 tbsp cocoa powder

Directions

1. Preheat your oven to 350 degrees F.
2. For the crust, get a medium bowl and whisk almond flour and salt in it. Add the oil and maple syrup to the bowl and mix to form a dough.
3. Separate the dough into two parts and press each into two small pie pans. Using a fork, make holes all over the doughs.
4. Transfer the pan to the oven and brown for about 15 minutes. After, take the pan out and let sit for a few minutes.
5. Except for the microgreens and strawberries, add every other ingredient for the filling into a blender and pulse. Spread the mixture onto your crust and add the microgreens and strawberries on top.

Nutritional Information

Calories: 797 Total Fat: 62.3 g Total Carbs: 44.1 g Protein: 21 g

Sheet Pan Fajitas with Bell Peppers and Chickpeas

Prep Time: 10 minutes

Cook Time: 20 minutes

Total Time: 30 minutes

Servings: 4

Ingredients

- Hot sauce
- 3 medium yellow bell peppers
- Fresh cilantro
- 2 cups cooked chickpeas
- 8 corn tortillas
- 1 medium yellow onion
- 3 tbsp olive oil
- ¼ tsp cumin
- 1 tbsp chili powder
- ½ tsp garlic powder
- 1 tsp fine sea salt

Directions

1. Preheat your oven to 450 degrees F. Line a baking sheet with parchment paper.
2. Mince the yellow onions and bell peppers and add them to the baking sheet. Also, add the chickpeas. Pour some oil on this mixture and sprinkle salt, chili, cumin, and garlic powder on it.
3. Toss well with clean hands and even them out.
4. Bake in the preheated oven for about 10 minutes. Take out the baking sheet, stir the ingredients, and return the pan to the oven for another 10 minutes.
5. Serve immediately with tortillas, hot sauce, and fresh cilantro.

Nutritional Information

Calories: 606 Total Fat: 18.5 g Total Carbs: 92.7 g Protein: 23.6 g

End of Summer Salad

Prep Time: 5 minutes

Cook Time: 5 minutes

Total Time: 10 minutes

Servings: 2

Ingredients

- 1 ½ tbsp mint, minced
- 3 ½ cups arugula microgreen
- 2 tbsp diced caper berries, remove the stems
- 1 cup ripe blackberries
- 1 crushed garlic clove
- 2 tbsp pine nuts
- 1 tbsp red wine vinegar
- 1 ear red corn, the cob removed
- 2 tbsp olive oil
- ½ bunch white asparagus
- Black pepper
- Sea salt

Directions

1. Rinse the arugula. Dry them and set aside.
2. Add oil, caper berries, vinegar, garlic, and mint to a small mixing bowl. Add a pinch of salt too. Mix and place the bowl in your refrigerator.
3. Cut off the ends of your asparagus, leaving the soft parts. Coat your spears with olive oil. Set your grill to medium heat and sear your asparagus. Sprinkle with salt and pepper and chop the asparagus into ½ inch pieces.
4. Get a large bowl and add the arugula, blackberries, asparagus, corn, and pine nuts. Add the salad dressing in the small bowl and serve immediately.

Nutritional Information

Calories: 265 Total Fat: 21.1 g Total Carbs: 19.7 g Protein: 5 g

Bacon Hash Brown Casserole with Eggs

Prep Time: 45 minutes

Cook Time: 35 minutes

Total Time: 1 hour 30 minutes

Servings: 6

Ingredients

- Handful minced microgreens
- 8 strips applewood smoked bacon
- 6 large eggs
- 4 cups peeled russet potatoes, grated
- Olive oil
- 1 cup yellow onion, grated
- 1 tbsp minced garlic
- 1 cup fresh breadcrumbs
- ¼ cup seeded and minced jalapeno peppers, wash and dry the peppers
- 1 ¼ tsp salt
- Freshly ground black pepper

Directions

1. Place a large saute pan over medium heat and add the bacon to it. Cook each side for 5 minutes, then take the bacon out. Place on a large plate lined with a paper towel. Don't discard the grease.
2. After grating the onions and potatoes, squeeze the liquid out of them. You want to get out as much liquid as you can, so take your time.
3. Preheat your oven to 375 degrees F.
4. Into the greasy pan, add jalapeno peppers, breadcrumbs, garlic, and the wrung out potatoes and garlic. Add olive oil, set the stove to medium-high heat, and cook for about 20 minutes. Stir occasionally. To prevent the potatoes from sticking to the bottom of the pan, you can add a bit of olive oil.
5. Crumble your bacon and put the pieces in the pan. Add salt and pepper, and stir.
6. Add the mixture in your pan to a 9x13 baking dish.
7. Press down with the back of a spoon to form an indent in the middle of the potato mixture.
8. Break your eggs into the dish, but space them out. Transfer the pan to your oven and bake for 20 minutes.
9. Finally, take the pan out of the oven and let sit for 10 minutes. Top with microgreens and serve.

Nutritional Information

Calories: 678 Total Fat: 49.2 g Total Carbs: 41.5 g Protein: 18.9 g

Microgreens with Strawberry-Lime Vinaigrette

Prep Time: 10 minutes

Cook Time: 0 minutes

Total Time: 10 minutes

Servings: 1

Ingredients

To make the salad:

- Strawberries cut in two
- 6 oz microgreens
- 2 minced radishes
- Fresh herb sprigs
- 12 minced snow peas

To make the vinaigrette:

- 3 tbsp olive oil
- 1 ½ cups chopped strawberries
- 2 tsp lime juice
- 2 tbsp white balsamic vinegar
- 1 tsp pure maple syrup

Directions

1. For the vinaigrette, add strawberries, maple syrup, and vinegar into a bowl and combine. Set aside for 30 minutes. Holding back the strawberries, pour the liquid into another small bowl. Add oil and lime juice into this second bowl and stir. Mix in salt and pepper.
2. For the salad, add the microgreens, radishes, ¼ of the vinaigrette, and snow peas into a bowl. Add the strawberries you reserved and toss. Top with sprigs and halved strawberries.

Nutritional Information

Calories: 105 Total Fat: 8 g Total Carbs: 9 g Protein: 1 g

Lemon and Pea Tendril Risotto

Prep Time: 5 minutes

Cook Time: 18 minutes

Total Time: 23 minutes

Servings: 2

Ingredients

- ¼ cup microgreens
- 3 peeled garlic cloves, minced
- 2 tbsp butter
- 2 oz pea tendrils, roughly chopped
- ⅓ cup parmesan cheese, grated
- 1 lemon
- Pinch saffron
- 1 deseeded red bell pepper, diced
- 3 tbsp vegetable demi-glace
- 1 cup bomba rice
- 1 yellow onion, peeled and diced

Directions

1. Peel the rind of the lemon and mince to get 2 tsp of zest. Seed the lemon and cut it into quarters.
2. Add 2 tsp of oil into a medium pot and place it over medium heat. Put salt, pepper, onion, and garlic into the pot and stir for 5 minutes.
3. Next, add the bell pepper and cook for 4 extra minutes.
4. Pour rice into the pot and set the heat to medium-high. Stir and cook for 2 minutes.
5. Add 3 ½ cups of water, vegetable demi-glace, lemon zest, lemon wedge juice, and saffron into the pot. Add some more salt and pepper if you wish. When the water starts to boil, turn the heat down to medium and cook for 16 minutes.
6. Turn off the heat and add butter, parmesan cheese, and the chopped tendrils.
7. Serve topped with pea tendrils, microgreens, and lemon wedges.

Nutritional Information

Calories: 198 Total Fat: 13 g Total Carbs: 18.5 g Protein: 5 g

Mediterranean Quinoa Salad

Prep Time: 5 minutes

Cook Time: 10 minutes

Total Time: 15 minutes

Servings: 2

Ingredients

For the salad:

- 2 cups microgreens
- 1 cup uncooked quinoa
- ½ chopped avocado
- 1 cup halved heirloom tomatoes
- 1 oz canned cooked black beans
- ½ cup pitted kalamata olives
- 2 ½ tbsp minced green onion

For the dressing:

- ½ cup olive oil
- 2 cloves large garlic
- ¼ cup fresh basil leaves
- ¼ cup red wine vinegar
- 1 tsp kosher salt
- 1 tsp black pepper

Directions

1. To make the dressing, put salt, basil, red wine vinegar, garlic, and pepper into a food processor. Slowly pour the oil while at high speed. Put the mixture into a bowl for later.
2. Cook quinoa according to the directions on the pack. Set aside to cool.

3. Afterward, add the remaining ingredients to the quinoa. Take the dressing out of the fridge and add 2 tbsp to the quinoa.
4. Serve immediately or store in your fridge.

Nutritional Information

Calories: 1002 Total Fat: 74.7 g Total Carbs: 72.1 g Protein: 18.9 g

Charred Rainbow Beet and Pistachio Salad

Prep Time: 10 minutes

Cook Time: 45 minutes

Total Time: 55 minutes

Servings: 2

Ingredients

- 2 small rainbow beets, scrubbed and trimmed
- Canola oil

For the basil olive oil:

- 2 cups basil, loosely packed
- 1 cup microgreens
- ¼ cup oil, scant
- 1 tbsp pistachios, chopped
- ½ cup lemon juice
- Pinch kosher salt
- Citrus herb salt

Directions

1. Place the ingredients for basil olive oil into a blender and pulse.
2. Toss the trimmed beets with 2 tsp of canola oil and place them on a baking sheet. Wrap with aluminum foil.
3. Set the grill to 350 degrees F and cook the beets for 45 minutes. Set the beets aside to cool.
4. Next, peel the skin off your beets and halve them.

5. Pour some of the basil olive oil onto 2 plates. Add ½ the microgreens and beets to each plate. Sprinkle with pistachio and herb salt. Top with what's left of the microgreens.
6. Serve immediately.

Nutritional Information

Calories: 346 Total Fat: 33.5 g Total Carbs: 14.6 g Protein: 2.5 g

Roasted Broccoli Microgreen Soup

Prep Time: 5 minutes

Cook Time: 25 minutes

Total Time: 30 minutes

Servings: 6

Ingredients

- 2 tbsp red balsamic vinaigrette
- 1 head broccoli, chopped
- 3 tbsp sunflower seeds, roasted
- 1 large minced onion
- 2 tbsp lemon juice
- 4 whole cloves garlic
- 1 cup cooked navy beans
- 1 tbsp olive oil
- 3 oz feta cheese
- 4 cups vegetable broth, low-sodium
- 1 cup sunflower shoots and 1 cup zesty mix microgreens
- ¼ salt
- ½ tsp chili powder

Directions

1. Place a rimmed baking sheet in your oven and preheat to 425 degrees F.
2. In a bowl, mix broccoli, oil, onion, salt, and garlic. Spread this mixture on your hot baking sheet and bake for 25 minutes.

3. Get a food processor and add the baked vegetables, lemon juice, broth, feta cheese, microgreens, beans, and chili powder. Pour this mixture into a saucepan and add a little water or broth. Warm the mixture.
4. Drizzle with vinaigrette and top with microgreens, cheese, and some sunflower seeds. Serve.

Nutritional Information

Calories: 309 Total Fat: 7.2 g Total Carbs: 47.2 g Protein: 15.2 g

Mushroom and Microgreen Omelet

Prep Time: 10 minutes

Cook Time: 0 minutes

Total Time: 10 minutes

Servings: 1

Ingredients

- 3 large eggs
- 1 tbsp unsalted butter
- ¾ cup microgreens
- 1 ½ oz minced white mushrooms
- Freshly ground pepper
- Coarse salt

Directions

1. Place a nonstick skillet on a stove set to medium-high heat. Melt ½ of the butter in the pan and cook the mushrooms for 2 minutes. Add salt and pepper, and stir.
2. Brown the mushrooms for 2 minutes and transfer into a small bowl. Add microgreens. Clean the skillet with paper towels.
3. Get a medium bowl and break the large eggs into it. Add salt and pepper and whisk. Put the remaining butter into the pan and melt. Cook the eggs without stirring. The omelet should set after 2 minutes, then add the cooked mushrooms and microgreens.
4. Serve immediately.

Nutritional Information

Calories: 322 Total Fat: 26.5 g Total Carbs: 2 g Protein: 19.8 g

Asparagus, Tomato, and Microgreen Salad

Prep Time: 15 minutes

Cook Time: 15 minutes

Total Time: 30 minutes

Servings: 6

Ingredients

To make the salad:

- ½ cup toasted slivered almonds
- ½ lb asparagus
- 4 cups arugula microgreens
- 2 small, diced Roma tomatoes

To make the dressing:

- 2 tbsp chopped parsley stem
- 1 medium grapefruit,
- 2 tbsp olive oil
- Pinch black pepper
- Pinch sea salt

Directions

1. Preheat your oven to 350 degrees F. Use aluminum foil to line a baking sheet. Add slivered almonds to the pan and bake for 7 minutes. Take the almonds out and set aside to cool.
2. Zest and juice the grapefruits, and add both into a small bowl. Mix and add parsley stems and oil. Whisk well and sprinkle in salt and pepper. This is the vinaigrette.
3. Boil a pot of water and cook the asparagus for 2 minutes. Take the vegetable out and keep in a bowl of ice water. Still crunchy, dry the asparagus and cut them into

1-inch pieces. Put them in a bowl and add chopped tomatoes and ½ vinaigrette. Toss.
4. Get another bowl. Add the remaining vinaigrette and microgreens. Add the asparagus mixture and serve.
5. Add toasted almonds as toppings.

Nutritional Information

Calories: 124 Total Fat: 9 g Total Carbs: 10.2 g Protein: 3.8 g

Kale and Radish Microgreen Salad

Prep Time: 10 minutes

Cook Time: 0 minutes

Total Time: 10 minutes

Servings: 2

Ingredients

- Pinch minced parsley
- Pack kale microgreens
- 1 julienned cucumber
- 1 chopped small red radish
- 1 julienned carrot
- 2 chopped small grape tomatoes
- 1 diced celery stalk

To make the dressing:

- 1 tsp lemon juice
- 2 tbsp aged balsamic vinegar
- 2 tbsp olive oil
- 1 tbsp avocado oil
- Pinch white pepper
- Pinch sea salt

Directions

1. Add the ingredients for the dressing into a small bowl and whisk thoroughly. Small balsamic balls will form in the mixture if you do this well.
2. In a 2:1 ratio, add the kale and radish microgreens on a flat plate. This ratio works well because radish has a stronger taste.
3. Place your cucumbers and carrots on the microgreens and, around the edges of these vegetables, add the slices of tomatoes, celery, and radish.
4. Sprinkle parsley and salt and drizzle with dressing over the veggies.
5. Serve.

Nutritional Information

Calories: 216 Total Fat: 15.3 g Total Carbs: 18.9 g Protein: 3.3 g

Seared Sea Scallops with Microgreen Salad

Prep Time: 5 minutes

Cook Time: 4 minutes

Total Time: 9 minutes

Servings: 4

Ingredients

- 1 tbsp olive oil
- 12 dry sea scallops
- 3 diced radishes
- 2 cups microgreen salad mix
- Freshly ground black pepper to taste
- Salt to taste

To make the miso and lime dressing:

- 1 tsp soy sauce, low-sodium
- 3 tbsp sweet white miso
- 3 tbsp fresh lime juice
- 2 tsp minced garlic
- 1 tbsp sesame oil
- 1 tbsp agave nectar

Directions

1. For the miso and lime, add soy sauce, white miso, garlic, agave, lime juice, and sesame oil into a small bowl. Pour in 3 tbsp of water and mix.
2. Cut out the still-attached side muscles of the scallops. Then, add salt and pepper to the scallops.
3. Put the microgreen mix and radishes into a different small bowl, and add 3 tbsp of the dressing. Toss and set aside. This is your salad.
4. Place a skillet over medium-high heat and pour in 1 tbsp of olive oil. Cook your scallops in the pan for 4 minutes. That's 2 minutes for each side.
5. Place the scallops on four plates and add the salad on each. Drizzle with what is left of your miso and lime dressing.
6. Serve immediately.

Nutritional Information

Calories: 201 Total Fat: 7.6 g Total Carbs: 16.3 g Protein: 17.2 g

Seared Halibut with Microgreens Salad

Prep Time: 25 minutes

Cook Time: 8 minutes

Total Time: 25 minutes

Servings: 4

Ingredients

- 6 cups assorted microgreens
- 2 peeled kiwi, chopped
- ⅓ cup torn fresh mint leaves, loosely packed
- ¼ cup chopped English cucumbers
- ⅓ cup torn fresh basil leaves, loosely packed
- 3 cups fresh strawberries, halved and minced
- ¼ tsp ground cinnamon
- 1 tbsp olive oil
- 4 6-oz halibut steaks, skin and bones removed
- Pinch ground cayenne pepper

- Pinch ground black pepper
- Pinch sea salt

Directions

1. Mix cucumber, lemon juice, kiwi, oil, strawberries, ½ salt, and black pepper into a small bowl. Let sit.
2. On every side of the halibut, rub with the remaining salt, cinnamon, black pepper, and cayenne.
3. Lightly coat a skillet with nonstick cooking spray and place the pan over medium-high heat. Cook the halibut in the skillet for 8 minutes. Turn the fish to make sure you get all sides. Turn off the heat and set the pan aside.
4. Into the strawberry mixture, mix the basil and mint.
5. Place microgreens on a plate, then add the halibut and basil mixture. Serve.

Nutritional Information

Calories: 312 Total Fat: 8 g Total Carbs: 54 g Protein: 39 g

Microgreen, Zucchini, and Carrot Cake

Prep Time: 6 minutes

Cook Time: 10 minutes

Total Time: 16 minutes

Servings: 4

Ingredients

- 1 tsp garlic powder
- 1 cup microgreens
- 2 tbsp chickpea
- 2 zucchinis
- 3 eggs
- 2 carrots
- 1 cup parmesan cheese, grated

Directions

1. Into a large bowl, shred the zucchini and carrots. Chop microgreens into the bowl and add parmesan cheese.
2. Break the eggs into a small bowl and add flour, salt, pepper, and garlic powder. Pour this into the large bowl and toss.
3. Add spoonfuls of this new mixture into an oiled sheet pan. With the back of the spoon, flatten the mixture into patties and bake for about 10 minutes. Serve.

Nutritional Information

Calories: 123 Total Fat: 5.4 g Total Carbs: 11.1 g Protein: 9.2 g

Super Microgreen Smoothie

Prep Time: 5 minutes

Cook Time: 0 minutes

Total Time: 5 minutes

Servings: 3

Ingredients

- 1 oz broccoli microgreens (kale is a good alternative)
- 1 diced banana
- 1 cup milk
- 5 large strawberries
- ¾ cups vanilla Greek yogurt
- Ice

Directions

1. Add all these ingredients into a blender and pulse until you get a smooth mixture. Serve.

Nutritional Information

Calories: 124 Total Fat: 2.5 g Total Carbs: 21.9 g Protein: 5.4 g

Blue Cheese Tomato with Microgreens

Prep Time: 10 minutes

Cook Time: 0 minutes

Total Time: 10 minutes

Servings: 4

Ingredients

- Handful microgreens
- 2 chopped, medium-sized ripe tomatoes
- 3 tbsp balsamic glaze
- ½ cup blue cheese, crumbled
- Salt and pepper to your taste

Directions

1. Place the tomato slices on a plate and sprinkle with salt, pepper, and cheese.
2. Drizzle glaze over the seasoned tomatoes and add microgreens as toppings. Serve.

Nutritional Information

Calories: 85 Total Fat: 5 g Total Carbs: 6 g Protein: 4 g

Cold Smoked Salmon Sandwiches with Microgreens

Prep Time: 15 minutes

Cook Time: 0 minutes

Total Time: 15 minutes

Servings: 4

Ingredients

- 3 small cress microgreens
- 6 slices soft wholemeal sandwich bread
- 14 minced cucumbers
- 100 g cold smoked salmon
- Butter

Direction

1. Spread butter on one side of each slice of bread.
2. Separate the microgreens, smoked salmon, and cucumber between the bread. Stack all the sandwiches together and cut them diagonally.

Nutritional Information

Calories: 140 Total Fat: 7 g Total Carbs: 21 g Protein: 8 g

Vegan Microgreen Soup

Prep Time: 5 minutes

Cook Time: 6 hours

Total Time: 6 hours 5 minutes

Servings: 4

Ingredients

- 2 carrots, chopped into small circles
- 1 tbsp olive oil
- 1 large cubed potato
- 1 medium onion, diced
- 1 tbsp dried parsley
- 2 chopped garlic cloves
- 8 oz cauliflower microgreens
- 2 chopped celery stalks
- 3 cups water
- 1 oz rum
- ½ tsp thyme
- 1 tsp salt

Directions

1. Put the oil in a pot and place it in a crock pot. If you don't have one, this soup can also be made in a coffee maker with a warming tray.
2. Cut onions, garlic, and celery into the pot. Pour rum into this mixture.

3. Add three cups of water to the crock pot and stir. If you're cooking in a coffee maker, add three cups of water and allow it to trickle through the machine, as this will heat the water up more quickly.
4. After an hour, add the microgreens and let cook for an additional hour.
5. Mix in salt and spices.
6. Add this mixture to your blender and puree until smooth.
7. Add carrots and potatoes to the pot. After cooking for 4 additional hours, serve.

Nutritional Information

Calories: 160 Total Fat: 3.5 g Total Carbs: 25 g Protein: 4 g

Conclusion

The microgreen stage is, arguably, the best time to consume vegetables. At this point in their development, the nutrient content and flavors of the greens are heightened. So, if you buy into the philosophy of eating your food as medicine, you should add microgreens to your diet.

They are also widely eaten now, so cultivating microgreens is commercially viable. Hopefully, this book has been useful in helping you successfully plant and harvest your microgreens. The materials needed to cultivate microgreens are relatively affordable and easy to set up. But the biggest incentive, some would say, is the fact that microgreens can, generally, be harvested in less than a month.

Microgreens can be used as a garnish or made into a smoothie. Refer to the recipes in this book as often as you need to for creative ideas on how to consume the greens.

References

Bliss, R. M. (2014). Specialty greens pack a nutritional punch. United States Department of Agriculture. https://agresearchmag.ars.usda.gov/2014/jan/greens

Choe, U., Yu, L. L., et al. (2018). The science behind microgreens as an exciting new food for the 21st century. *National Library of Medicine 66(44),* 11519-11530. doi: 10.1021/acs.jafc.8b03096

Huang, H., Jiang, X., et al. (2016). Red cabbage microgreens lower circulating low-density lipoprotein (LDL), liver cholesterol, and inflammatory cytokines in mice fed a high-fat diet. *National Library of Medicine 64(48),* 9161-9171. doi: 10.1021/acs.jafc.6b03805

Patil, B. (2016). Vegetable and fruit improvement center. Texas A&M Agrilife Research. https://vfic.tamu.edu/

Book 2: Hydroponic Gardening for Beginners:

A How-To Guide for Growing Vegetables, Herbs & Fruits in Your Own Sustainable Soil-Free Home Hydroponic Garden

Basil Green

Bonus!

Wouldn't it be nice to have even more motivation and inspiration on your gardening journey? As a sincere "Thank you" for reading my book, i've given you access to a FREE Indoor Gardening ebook below!

Go to This Link to Get Your Free Bonus Indoor Gardening Ebook:

bit.ly/Indoorgardeningfree

These indoor gardening tips helped me immensely with my indoor growing. I hope they help you too!

Introduction

Okay, so you've heard about hydroponics, but what is it and why would you want to try it?

Hydroponics is not a new-age concept, it has been around for a long time, but it is growing in popularity for its soil-free, space-saving, and water benefits. It's not even that difficult to get started with. Kids can do it! You don't need a lot of space, or a garden; it requires no soil. All you need is the time and patience it takes to read this book and you will be well on your way to getting started with your own home hydroponic gardening system.

Hydroponics is a varied genre of horticulture. There are different systems to match different levels of experience and knowledge, right from the absolute beginner to the veteran gardener and even the tech-savvy gardener. There are basic systems you can make from common household items or materials you have lying around the home and garage to fancy systems that require a decent amount of technical know-how. In this book, we will cover all these systems and explain how you can choose and make one of the four simpler systems suitable for beginners.

From page one, we will arm you with all the information you need:

- Understanding the concept of hydroponics and what it is.
- Why it's a great option for urban gardeners.
- How hydroponics is paving the way for the future of agriculture.
- What the different hydroponic systems are.
- How to make your own hydroponic gardening system at home and some handy tips to help you along the way.

So, now ask yourself this. Are you ready to be stuck in on your journey of growing delicious herbs, vegetables, and fruits right in your own home or garden? If you answered 'yes,' then keep reading as we guide you to your goal every step of the way.

Chapter 1

Hydroponic Gardening: A History and Overview

What Is Hydroponic Gardening?

Hydroponic gardening is often referred to simply as hydroponics. It is a subdivision of what is called hydroculture. Hydroculture is a way of growing plants where they are not grown in soil. Grow plants without soil? That's right! As much as the traditional concept of your hands in the earth and growing plants in soil comes to mind when you think about gardening, you can successfully grow plants out of soil. Instead of soil, hydroponics uses a solution of mineral nutrients dissolved in water to provide the plants with the essential nutrients they need. There are various ways of doing this. Often, the roots are directly exposed to the solution or an immobile substrate other than soil may support them.

Nutrients from a variety of sources may be used in hydroponic systems. Some examples may include chemical fertilizers, duck manure, and artificial nutrients in solutions. Where you get your nutrients from will depend on the type of system you use and what is most readily available to you.

Hydroponics is versatile and allows you to grow a variety of different plants from vegetables, to herbs, to flowers, and even marijuana! A hydroponic garden offers various advantages but comes with its disadvantages as well, all of which we will cover in later sections of this book.

The Beginnings of Hydroponic Gardening

Let's start by dissecting the word hydroponics. It is derived from two root words. The first word is 'hydro', which is English and relates to water. The second root word is 'ponos' which is Greek and relates to work, effort, or labor. Therefore, hydroponics means working with water in a soilless environment to grow plants.

Many people think that hydroponics is a relatively new concept. It may seem futuristic in comparison to the age-old traditional method of growing plants that have been employed since humans discovered agriculture. The truth, though, is actually quite different.

Hydroponic gardening has been around for thousands of years. The ancient world is where it all began. Around 500 B.C.E. King Nebuchadnezzar II gifted his wife, Amytis, with the Hanging Gardens of Babylon, one of the seven wonders of the ancient world. Archeologists and scholars alike have studied the intricate watering systems that supported these legendary gardens for a long time. The way they worked was elevated stonework supporting the plants with central water reservoirs allowing water to flow down over their roots, providing nutrients and aeration. While the hanging gardens are still but a legend, not having yet been discovered by archeologists, their description is clearly an example of hydroponics.

A later example of hydroponic gardening comes in the form of the floating gardens of China, as described by Marco Polo when he documented his travels in the 1300s. Rice is an age-old example of hydroponics as it is grown in water. Initial attempts to grow rice in soil, while difficult, it wasn't unsuccessful. Seasonal floods would decimate other subsistence crops, but rice withstood the waterlogged conditions, and it began to thrive in them. That is where the hydroponic farming of rice paddies in organized fields began. When hydroponic rice farming took off, the rice not only thrived, it also became resistant to more diseases that could possibly plague it, making it hardy and yielding better crops. That's not where the orient stopped with their hydroponics. When Marco Polo documented the use of hydroponics in China, they had developed it to use in growing ornamental gardens.

Hydroponics didn't just stop at providing hardy rice crops; it led to the development of aquaponics. Aquaponics is a system whereby a hydroponic system doesn't just provide a crop harvest above the water; it also supports the farming of fish below the water. Aquaponics has two applications. The first is ornamental, where plants are grown on top of the water. Fishes such as koi are kept in water in spaces like gardens. The other is where crops are grown on the surface and edible fish are farmed below the surface, providing two different sources of food in one body of water.

Another civilization that made use of hydroponics for growing crops is the Aztecs in the 14th to 16th century C.E. The swamp-like regions they lived in, as well as their nomadic way of life, meant that traditional field farming of crops wasn't possible. Instead, they built large floating rafts out of reeds tethered together with dried roots, which would float in the canals surrounding their communities. They would then dredge up silt from the bottom of the canal, which was rich in nutrients, and lay that on top of the rafts. The crops are grown on the rafts and their roots would push through into the water.

As you can see, people have been using soilless systems to grow plants and crops for a long time. However, while there is further documentation of hydroponics throughout history, it wasn't until relatively recently in our modern history that it came to prominence around the world. It wasn't until much later that the concept became popular and intensive research began in order to understand and diversify that concept into what we know today.

In modern times, the earliest recorded reference made to hydroponics was by William Frederick Gericke. In the early part of the 20th century, he started popularizing the concept of growing plants without soil but using water instead. At the time, he was working at the University of California and both his colleagues and the general public were skeptical about his concept of hydroponics. He would go on to prove his claims to be right when he successfully used only water and nutrients to grow 25-foot high tomato vines. He named his concept hydroponics. Since then the concept and application of hydroponics for a variety of purposes, specifically agriculture, has been intensively researched and developed.

Hydroponics for the Future

Hydroponics is increasingly becoming a viable, if not the most viable, way of farming and growing crops. This is because as our global population grows, the amount of usable land for agriculture is declining. Food demands are going up, but the ability to keep up with the demand is slowly declining by the year.

Hydroponic farming allows for the better utilization of space, just like it does with gardening. Farmers will be able to produce more food more efficiently through vertical crop farming, making the most out of less space. This theory can also be applied to your garden in terms of urban farming on a small scale. You rely less on commercial farming when you grow your own vegetables and plants, and just like commercial farming, you can use less space to grow more. This allows you to utilize every bit of space, even vertically, that you have available to you, providing you and your family with delicious, homegrown vegetables.

The other benefit of hydroponics is that it doesn't use nearly as much water as traditional farming and gardening. As our world becomes more populated and more polluted, usable water resources become less. With hydroponics, water is efficiently used and conserved, using less of our precious drinking water supplies as they become scarcer into the future.

Interestingly, NASA is investigating the use of hydroponics to grow fresh food for astronauts in space. Hydroponics could be taking subsistence gardening out of this world.

Advantages of Hydroponic Gardening

As with most things in the world, hydroponics comes with its advantages and disadvantages. Here's what you need to know about the advantages of hydroponic gardening.

No Soil Necessary

Hydroponics work on a soilless system of growing plants. When you don't need soil to grow plants, you can grow plants, such as agricultural crops, in areas that are otherwise unsuitable. It may be because there isn't space, the soil doesn't have enough nutrients, or the land that is available is contaminated.

Space-Saving

When you grow plants in soil, their roots will spread out as they seek food and oxygen. Hydroponics provides a nutrient-rich, oxygenated solution straight to the roots of the plant, meaning that they don't have to expand or compete with each other for nutrients. Hydroponic arrangements allow plants to be planted much closer together, saving space and allowing more plants to grow in the same amount of space.

Natural Elements Aren't a Problem Indoors

When you grow plants outside, they are exposed to elements. Indoor hydroponics has similar advantages to soil-based greenhouses in that you have complete control over the climate your plants are growing in. You can control the temperature, composition of the air, light, and humidity. This allows you to grow plants out of season.

Water-Wise Growing

It's no secret that hydroponic gardening saves water by using only around 10% of the amount of water that traditional soil-based growing uses. Water is used sparingly in many recirculating systems, which means that the plants only take up what they need. The rest runs off, is collected, and the water is circulated back into the system. The only two ways water is lost in these hydroponic gardening setups is through minimal evaporation or leaks in the system.

Nutrients

When you grow plants in soil, depending on the type of plants, only certain nutrients are used, while others aren't. If you plant the same crops or plants repeatedly, the soil becomes depleted of the necessary nutrients for that crop. This is how crop rotation developed. On the other hand, when you use hydroponics you have complete control over what nutrients you put into the solution. You can find out what nutrients are needed for particular plants and how much they need and calculate how much to add to your solution at specific stages of growth. You also don't have the same nutrient loss or change as with soil.

pH Control

Balancing the pH levels in the soil is much more difficult. Using hydroponics, you are able to control the pH levels based on the mineral content of the water, making absorption more efficient.

Plants Grow Faster

When you can control every aspect of an indoor environment that plants grow in, you can create the ideal environment for those plants to grow optimally without much work from the plant. Plants grown with indoor hydroponics don't have to expend precious energy in searching for nutrients and dealing with temperature and light fluctuations. Instead, they can put all their energy into growing.

No Weed Woes

Soil is prone to the annoyance of weeds popping up. Without soil, there are no weeds and no plowing, tilling, etc.

Diseases and Pest Problems Are Less

Hydroponic gardening in a closed and controlled environment lessens the number of pests and diseases associated with soil-grown plants are reduced. If they can't get in or they can't be transferred via soil, they can't be a menace to your gardening. Outdoor hydroponic systems may be somewhat more susceptible to certain pests and diseases compared to indoor systems but without the presence of soil, they are still less prone to diseases than traditional gardening.

Be Gone Herbicides a Pesticides

Since you are removing soil from the equation, many pests and diseases, as well as weeds, associated with traditional gardening are greatly minimized or removed altogether. This means that you don't have to rely on pesticides and herbicides as much as with traditional soil-based gardening. This reduces the amount of harmful chemicals being applied to your plants.

Less Labor, Less Time

With a soilless system, you cut out or minimize tilling, weeding, watering, applying pesticides, manually ridding your garden of pests, testing soil quality, fertilizing, and watering. This, overall, saves you a lot of time and effort.

A Great Hobby

Just as with traditional gardening, hydroponic gardening is a great hobby that allows you to commune with nature. Gardening is a form of therapeutic stress relief, and it offers you tasty rewards when you grow your own veggies!

So, we have extolled the virtues of hydroponic gardening, but what about the negatives that accompany every positive?

Disadvantages of Hydroponic Gardening

It Needs Your Time

Although hydroponics is less labor-intensive and does save time in comparison to traditional gardening, it will still take up some of your time. After all, you are still growing life, tending to it, and cultivating it to be the best it can be. Hydroponics also, unlike their soil-grown counterparts, cannot be left unattended for days or even weeks on end. They need constant care because your system will only keep them going for a short period of time.

Commitment Is Key

You have to be committed to make a hydroponic garden work. You can't leave it alone and hope for the best. You need to learn how it works, discover the nuances about each plant you are growing, and the specific care they need. You have to be committed to being a plant parent and looking after them like a child would need looking after.

Knowledge and Experience

Just as with gardening in soil, hydroponics requires knowledge and experience. You will need to learn how to set up, use, and maintain your equipment. You will have to learn about your plants and their needs and calculate the nutrients, light, temperature, humidity, and more that they will need for optimum growth and health. You will learn through trial and error, and you will gain experience to make you more successful going forward.

Organic or Not Organic, That Is the Question

It is a hotly debated subject whether plants grown using hydroponics are organic or not. The microbiomes that are found in soil may not be the same as with hydroponic systems.

Energy and Water

When using a hydroponic gardening system, water and electricity are used. It is a good idea to make sure everything is set up properly to avoid dangerous situations when water and electricity are in close proximity to one another.

Systems Sometimes Fail

A backup power source is sometimes a good idea when you are using hydroponics for gardening. Depending on how your system is set up, a power outage of several hours could put your plants in jeopardy.

Start-Up Costs

Hydroponic gardening isn't a cheap venture when you really get into it. It takes time and money to set up a good system. Depending on how big or fancy you are going, it could cost hundreds to several thousands of dollars to set your system up. You have the framework, the electrical wiring and pumps, lighting, temperature control, humidity control, and more to budget into the cost of starting up. To start, the costs of basic systems can be quite low. You might even be able to make one using what you have at home, but a solid system for a committed grower is going to cost more. Once set up, your system won't be as costly to maintain, but the initial investment is worth consideration.

Close Quarters

When plants grow in close proximity to each other, which is the space-saving aspect of a hydroponic system, the spread of disease and potential pests is faster than with traditional gardening. We will provide information on pest and disease control for hydroponic gardening later in this book.

Chapter 2

Practices of Hydroponic Gardening

Water Culture vs Medium Culture

When it comes to hydroponics, there are two main categories to choose from. Water culture and medium culture. Water culture is where there is little to no growing medium, such as soil, which is used for growing plants. The plants are fed an artificial nutrient solution straight to the roots. In medium culture, some form of solid medium, not soil though, is used to grow the plants.

Water Culture

The name water culture can be deceiving. You are not just growing your plants with water but rather a nutrient-rich solution made with water. Another term might be solution culture, but water culture seems to be the one that sticks. There are various types of water culture, but the first decision to make is static water culture or continuous-flow water culture systems. The difference between these two systems is that in a static water culture system the nutrient solution doesn't move and stays in place, while in a recirculating water culture system the solution is constantly on the move. Let's take a closer look at the two methods.

Static Water Culture

When we speak of static water culture, we are talking about a hydroponics practice whereby plants are grown in reservoirs that are filled with a man-made nutrient solution. The point of the static solution culture is the word static. The plants are grown in the reservoir where the solution is kept. They are not grown in a container separate from the reservoir, as is the case with continuous-flow systems. The water is not on the move, so it is not misted, dripped, or flowing over the plant roots and then being recirculated through an external reservoir or allowed to run-to-waste.

Continuous-Flow Water Culture

A continuous-flow water culture is a system whereby the solution is on the move and not static. Plants are grown in containers, which are separate from the reservoir where the solution is kept. The solution can be dripped, misted, or applied to the roots in various ways, but the key point is that the water is moving. This means that continuous-flow culture can be part of a run-to-waste (RTW) system or a recirculating system.

Medium Culture

While hydroponics is known as a soilless way of growing plants, it doesn't mean that a substrate other than soil can't be used. These are known as growing mediums, and various hydroponic systems make use of these substrates. The substrates aid hydroponics in three ways.

Substrates are made of loose particles. As the plant roots grow, they grow between the particles, similar to how plants grow in soil. If you've ever pulled a plant up out of the ground, roots and all, you will notice that it often brings with it clumps of soil. This is because the roots have grown between the soil particles and the finer parts of the root system have trapped the soil particles like a mesh net. What this does when roots grow between substrate particles is that it helps to aerate the roots, offering them ample opportunities to get enough oxygen.

Substrates retain moisture. Even if the solution has been passed through the substrate, it will retain some of that solution, providing plants with the opportunity to draw that nutrient-rich solution from the substrate continuously. It also helps to keep the plant roots damp, stopping them from potentially drying out. Again, this emulates the way plants grow in soil. When you water your garden or houseplants, the water passes through the soil, but the soil retains some of the water for them to draw up over time.

Finally, substrates help to insulate your plant's roots. This is important because it protects them from heat, which could potentially damage them.

What Are the Hydroponic Growing Mediums?

Rockwool

One of the more popular growing mediums, rockwool, is non-degradable and made up of mainly granite but may contain limestone as well. These are superheated until they melt and then they are spun into thin, wool-like threads similar to cotton candy or sheep's wool.

Caution: When using rockwool, ensure that it never becomes saturated. It soaks up water fast and could suffocate your roots or cause stem and root rot. Rockwool needs to be pH balanced, so soak it in some pH-balanced water before you use it.

Hydrocorn

Hydrocorn is also known as grow rock and it is a lightweight expanded clay aggregate (LECA). This means that clay that has been super-fired in order to create porousness. It's lightweight enough so that it doesn't squash your plant roots but at the same time heavy enough to offer support. Hydrocorn has a neutral pH balance and is ideal for both retaining moisture and wicking moisture upwards towards plant roots. This growing medium is reusable, but you will have to clean and sterilize it before reuse.

Coco Fiber/Coco Chips

Coco fiber, also known as coco coir, and coco chips are made from outside husks of coconuts. Even though coco fiber is an organic, biodegradable product, it does so very slowly, and it won't contribute any nutritional value for your plants. It retains water well and is pH balanced. The difference between coco fiber and coco chips is the size of the substrate particles. The particle size of coco fiber is roughly the same as potting soil, while coco chips are roughly the size of wood chips. The benefit of coco chips is that their larger size offers better aeration at the root level.

Perlite

Perlite is primarily made up of minerals that have been significantly heated until they expand almost like how heated corn kernels pop into popcorn. This means that this substrate is lightweight, porous and absorbs liquid well. Not only does it retain water well, but it also acts as a good wicking agent. Because perlite is so lightweight, it floats and thus is not the best option for ebb and flow hydroponic systems.

Caution: Wet perlite down before you work with it so that the dust doesn't become airborne and get into your eyes.

Vermiculite

Similar to perlite, vermiculite is a silicate mineral. Likewise, it is heated and expands. Vermiculite is very similar to perlite in its ability to store nutrients to be used later. Just like perlite, it is very lightweight and not suitable for ebb and flow systems.

Caution: Vermiculite comes in different types for different uses. Be sure to use the type that is intended for use in horticulture.

Oasis Cubes

Similar to rockwool cubes and having similar properties but not appearance, oasis cubes are more akin to white or green floral foam. The material is what is called open-celled, which means that the cells can absorb air and liquid. It is also a good wicking agent and because of the open cells, the roots of the plants can easily expand and grow. Oasis cubes are traditionally used as a start to growing plants in hydroponics but can be used as substrate as well.

Caution: As with rockwool, oasis cubes absorb water quickly and easily, so be careful not to saturate them so that you won't suffocate the plant roots or end up with stem and root rot.

Floral Foam

Similar to oasis cubes, floral foam is an open-cell growing medium. However, the size of the cells is larger than oasis cubes. You may enter a few problems if you are going to use floral foam. It crumbles easily which can cause particles to get into your nutrient solution and contaminate your reservoir if you have a recirculating system. Like oasis cubes and rockwool, you don't want it to become saturated. It will have the same effect of suffocating your roots or causing root and stem rot.

Growstone

Recycled glass is used to make growstone. It is dust-free and lightweight. It also provides good aeration to the roots by creating large air pockets between the stones. Growstones are porous and offer a good wicking capability. Being able to wick water up to four inches above the waterline means that you will want good drainage in place or a deep layer of this substrate.

River Rock

River rock is easy to find and a common product in home improvement stores and pet supply stores. It is a relatively cost-effective substrate option. They do not retain water well as they are not porous, and their size provides many large air pockets between the rocks. You will want to feed often with your nutrient solution so that the plant roots don't dry out.

Caution: If you are using river rock as a substrate, try mixing in coco chips to help with moisture retention and minimize the drying of roots.

Pine Shavings

Inexpensive and utilized by many commercial growers, pine shavings are a good option for bigger home hydroponic gardening setups. As pine shavings are wood, they have good absorption but can easily become waterlogged.

Caution: Ensure that you use pine shavings and not sawdust. Also, make sure that the source is kiln-dried wood and that it does not have any chemical fungicides in it. Make sure that the pine shavings have good drainage and don't become waterlogged or you could end up with root problems.

Aged Composted Pine Bark

Pine bark is often considered a better option than many other tree bark substrates. It doesn't decompose as quickly and easily and contains a lesser amount of organic acids, which could possibly contaminate your nutrient solution.

Polyurethane Foam

Not commonly used in hydroponic gardening, polyurethane foam can sometimes be used as an alternative to rockwool. It is cost-effective and not hard to come by; it is often called foam batting.

Water-Absorbing Crystals

Water-absorbing crystals are not new and are not common for hydroponics. Polymer crystals that absorb water are used in many applications. One application has been in traditional gardening where these crystals are mixed into the soil to help with moisture retention. They expand greatly, and as much as 50 gallons of water can be retained in only one pound of crystals. They come in a variety of sizes from resembling a powder to the size of a marble, or the size of a golf ball. Depending on how big the crystals are, they can take up to two hours to absorb their full amount of water. They resemble jello when they are saturated. They are reusable once completely dried out and can then be easily stored.

Caution: When used on their own, because of their expansion and moldable nature when they are saturated, these crystals could cause problems with providing an adequate oxygen supply to roots.

Sand

Not to be confused with soil, sand is a common growing medium for hydroponic gardening. Similar to rock, the only difference being its tiny pint-sized particles, it doesn't drain water as quickly. You can easily, and this is common practice when using sand as a substrate, mix it with the likes of coco fiber, perlite, and vermiculite.

Tip: Use the largest size of sand grain you can find as this increases aeration.

Caution: Sand can be very heavy as a growing medium for hydroponic gardening. Mixing it with other substrates helps lessen the load but always be careful.

Rice Hulls

Your location will dictate whether rice hulls are easily accessible. Being an organic substrate isn't a problem as rice hulls degrade very slowly. Rice hulls are commonly added to a mix of growing mediums as opposed to being used as a stand-alone substrate. They generally have the correct pH-balance, which is a bonus.

Caution: Ensure that you use parboiled rice husks (PRH) because when it is fresh it could contain contaminating pathogens.

Irrigation and Feeding Techniques

In this section, we will discuss the two types of irrigation: run-to-waste and recirculating. These irrigation techniques don't necessarily have anything to do with how the nutrient solution is provided to the plants, such as dripping or misting, but rather with how the solution is managed. In addition to solution management irrigation practices, we will also discuss sub-irrigation and top-feeding irrigation.

Sub-Irrigation

As the name implies, sub-irrigation is the method of providing a nutrient solution to your plants from below. Examples of hydroponic systems, which make use of sub-irrigation are deep water culture, ebb and flow, nutrient film technique, and the wick system. In these systems, the nutrient solution is provided to the plants from below. The plant roots rest in the solution or the solution is transferred upwards towards the roots through the substrate. The key is that the solution is provided at or below the root level.

Passive Sub-Irrigation

Passive sub-irrigation is also known as semi-hydroponics or passive hydroponics. It uses a substrate to grow the plants in. These substrates are porous and allow water to be transferred upwards to the plant roots. A separate reservoir is used for the nutrient solution, placed below the substrate so that the roots are not directly in contact with the solution. Passive sub-irrigation is a form of static solution culture.

A simple but effective example of passive sub-irrigation is to use a substrate or growing medium, such as grow rock, which is porous and has a good wicking capability. Take a plastic soda bottle and cut it horizontally in half. Fill half of the bottom half of the bottle with a nutrient solution. Remove the cap and flip the top half of the bottle upside down. Insert a wicking material to use as a wick, such as cutting a cotton sock into strips, through the upside-down bottleneck so that half the wick strips are inside the bottle and the other half is sticking out the bottleneck. Place the upside-down top half of the bottle into the bottom half, fill it with your substrate, sow your plant and start growing. The solution will be transferred to the substrate by the wicks and then the substrate will carry it further up to the plant roots.

Top-Feeding Irrigation

In a top-feeding irrigation system, the nutrient solution is provided to the plants from above the root level. Hydroponic systems that use this type of irrigation include drip systems and top-feeding deep water culture systems. The solution is applied from above and moves downwards, often through a growing medium or substrate.

Run-to-Waste

Run-to-waste (RTW) in a hydroponic system, also called feeding-to-waste or drain-to-waste, is exactly what it sounds like. In this irrigation practice, plants are typically grown in a substrate with good liquid retention capabilities. The nutrient solution is passed along through the substrate and excess solution runs off or drains to 'waste' in a catchment container separate from the reservoir. This is a concept similar to how soil functions. Water passes through the soil, allowing plants to absorb water as it passes the roots. The run-to-waste irrigation practice may seem wasteful, as the name implies, but it does have both advantages and disadvantages.

Advantages:

- Nutrients don't become depleted in the solution because a fresh solution is provided with each feeding. This means you do not have to monitor the reservoir solution's nutrient levels or top them up.
- The electroconductivity (EC) of the nutrient solution in the reservoir remains constant.
- The pH balance of the solution remains constant.
- The maintenance of a run-to-waste irrigation system is lower than a nutrient recirculating system.
- The solution is not as prone to a build-up of pathogens such as bacteria.
- The liquid retention capability of the substrate used keeps the roots of the plants moist and thus helps guard your plants against an electrical failure, which could disable the solution supply.
- The substrate acts as insulation, protecting the plant roots against heat.

Disadvantages:

- Uses more water.
- Uses more nutrients, which adds to the costs.
- Nutrient leaching may happen more frequently.
- You may experience salt accumulation.
- This irrigation practice is only applicable to some hydroponic systems.

Recirculating Your Nutrient Solution

The opposite of run-to-waste is recirculating your nutrient solution. In a recirculating system, the plants are provided with the nutrient solution. The excess that runs off is then recaptured and circulated back into the reservoir to be used again. This may seem like a smarter practice than run-to-waste but there are both positives and negatives.

Advantages:

- The nutrient solution is recycled, losing less water and nutrients.
- Nutrient leaching is reduced.
- The amount of nutrients you use may be reduced.
- Several hydroponic systems may be run on a recirculating irrigation practice.

Disadvantages:

- Water-borne diseases are more common and spread like wildfire.
- Nutrient levels of the solution will fluctuate as plants absorb the nutrients in the quantities they need. This leads to the solution becoming depleted, which will require constant testing and management of nutrient levels.
- The pH and electroconductivity of the solution may fluctuate which will require testing to manage and maintain at appropriate levels.
- Algae growth is more likely, and drip emitters may become blocked with biofilm or algae.

Chapter 3

Understanding Hydroponic Systems

Before we get into the different hydroponic systems and how they work, let's start with a quick guide on how to germinate the seeds into the seedlings you will be planting in these systems.

Germinating Seeds Without Soil

The simplest and most convenient way to get seedlings for your hydroponic system is to go to the local nursery and buy seedlings that have already been germinated and have started growing. There are three drawbacks to this approach.

- You haven't had control over the quality of nutrients the seedlings have received from day one, so you haven't been able to control whether they got the best start in life or not.
- You may be quite limited in what you can grow according to what seedlings are available.
- Let's face it, that sense of pride and self-satisfaction that you get from germinating your own seeds is worth the effort, and you really don't get that from buying seedlings.

Okay, so we've convinced you to give germinating your own seedlings a try. Now, how do you do it?

- Choose your germinating medium. The two most popular choices are coco peat and rockwool cubes. Both are good choices for germinating seeds with a neutral pH and a good water to oxygen ratio.
- Once you have chosen your germinating medium, prep it by letting it stand for a few hours in distilled water.
- Drain excess water out of your germinating medium by lightly shaking it.
- Place a few seeds into your medium. You want to use a few seeds per piece of germinating medium in case some don't sprout. If you want to, you can always separate or remove any extra sprouts later.

- Put your growing medium in a shallow container with a cover. Set it aside in a safe, dark place until sprouting begins, which usually starts in about five to seven days.
- During the germination phase, ensure that the germinating medium stays damp but not drenched. If it is too wet, it will be soggy and fall apart. Keeping it at the right moisture level will help get the best germination results. Start off with distilled water. You can begin adding small amounts of nutrients later on or you can wait until your seedlings reach a height of two inches. After, start providing the mix of nutrient solution you would feed adult plants that has been quite diluted. If you test the EC of the seedling solution, it shouldn't have a reading above 8-1.2.
- Once your seeds have germinated, they will enter the propagation stage where they start growing and becoming stronger. Once your seedlings have developed stronger roots and about three sets of proper leaves, they are ready to be transplanted into your hydroponic system where they will live out the rest of their lives.

Tips

- Don't let the germinating medium dry out.
- Don't let the germination container be affected by extremes in temperature variations. Research what temperatures are best for germinating the seeds you are going to grow and try to keep the container at that general temperature.
- After transplanting your seedlings into your hydroponic gardening system, water them with nutrient solution from the top for a week or so to allow the roots to grow downward and prevent drying out.

The Six Main Hydroponic Systems

In hydroponics, there are six main systems. Each system has its benefits and drawbacks. To choose the right system for your needs and the plants you want to grow, you need to understand how each system works.

Wick System

The wick system is one of the simplest hydroponics systems and it is a good place for beginners to start. It is known as a passive system, meaning that there are no moving parts to this system. Passive sub-irrigation is what the wick system makes use of for irrigating your plants. The plants are grown in a container filled with substrate above the reservoir, and there are wicks that hang down from the substrate container into the reservoir. The wicks carry the nutrient solution up to the substrate or growing medium, which is where the plants then draw their nutrients and water from.

A wick system is the simplest hydroponic system by far and can be seen as a training stepladder to bigger and better systems. It is so easy that you can literally make it out of ordinary household items or by upcycling or recycling items you would otherwise normally chuck in the trash.

The one thing to consider in your setup is whether you are going to use an air pump or not. It is an optional addition to your wick system, so it isn't necessary, but it can be beneficial. Your plants should be able to take up oxygen from the air pockets in the substrate it's planted in and from the water the nutrients are mixed with. However, providing more oxygen isn't a bad idea. Not only does using an air pump boost the oxygen level on the solution, it also helps keep the solution swirling and moving. This constantly mixes up the nutrients and prevents them from setting at the bottom of the reservoir.

Advantages of the wick system:

- It is easy and cost-effective to build.
- It is easy to maintain, making it ideal for beginners.
- It doesn't require large energy inputs.

Disadvantages of the wick system:

- Unsuitable for larger plants that need to draw up more water.
- Nutrient delivery isn't very efficient. The wicks can't tell how much of what nutrients the plant needs and just transports everything equally to the growing medium. The plant takes up as much of the necessary nutrients as it needs and leaves the rest behind in the substrate, which can cause a potentially toxic buildup of nutrients.

What to Grow

A wick system is a good idea if you are planting small, non-fruit-bearing plants. This system cannot support water-hungry plants or plants that need larger amounts of nutrients. It cannot supply enough water and nutrients to those plants and it cannot do so quickly enough.

Your best plant choices are plants that are relatively small in size, light on water and nutrients such as lettuces and herbs.

Deep Water Culture

Deep water culture (DWC), also referred to as direct water culture, and is a system of hydroponics where your plants are suspended over a reservoir of a well-oxygenated nutrient solution. The roots of the plant are submerged in the solution. There are two reasons this system got its name. Firstly, the reservoir used should be able to hold a fair amount of solution. Secondly, much of your plant root mass is constantly submerged in the solution almost all day long. This is unlike other systems, which may wet or drench the roots several times a day, leaving the roots exposed to the moisture-retaining substrate in between.

Deep water culture is a popular hydroponics system for beginners as it is relatively easy and inexpensive to set up and use. The only hydroponics system that is even easier and simpler to use is the wick system.

Advantages of Deep Water Culture:

- Once you are set up, this system is quite low maintenance.
- Compared with traditional soil growing, a deep water culture system allows plants to grow much faster.
- Putting together a deep water culture system is easy, and there are relatively few moving parts involved.

Disadvantages of Deep Water Culture:

Some disadvantages may be circumnavigated through proper hydroponic garden maintenance.

- Fluctuations in pH, nutrient concentration, and the level of the solution in the reservoir can fluctuate greatly in smaller systems.
- If you are working with a smaller system, due to the small scale of the system, it can either be extremely easy to under or over calibrate your nutrient solution.
- If your air pump fails or you have an electricity outage, the roots of your plants may 'drown' if there isn't enough oxygen being pumped into the solution.
- Maintaining a constant water temperature can be a bit of a headache.

Variations

When it comes to deep water culture systems, there is more than one to choose from to suit your specific growing needs.

Traditional Deep Water Culture

A traditional deep water culture system is often where newcomers to hydroponics start out. These systems are easy to set up, easy to maintain, and don't break the bank. They also offer you the option to expand at a later stage into a modular or recirculating deep water system. These systems utilize either a floating raft concept or gaps for plant containers that are cut into the container lid. Plants are placed in holders or on the raft with their roots suspended in the nutrient solution. An air pump and air stone aerate the water that prevents plant suffocation. The advantage of opting to go with the floating raft concept is that as the water level drops, so does the raft, which ensures that your plant roots are always suspended in the solution. If you opt for placing plant holders in the lid of the container, pay careful attention to the level of the solution so that it does not drop lower than the roots can reach.

Static vs Recirculating

This question is the same as asking whether you should have a singular or modular deep water system. The answer is simple. If you are new to hydroponics, it's best to start simple with a singular or static system. A singular or static system is one in which each plant or cluster of plants is in its own reservoir of nutrient solution, separate from other plants or plant clusters and reservoirs. You may have multiple reservoirs to grow multiple plants or plant clusters at the same time, but they are all separate from each other. This does bring in a bit more work because each separate reservoir needs to be tested for pH and nutrient concentration.

Modular or recirculating deep water systems link several containers with the same type of plants together and to a central reservoir. The nutrient solution is then circulated through all the containers and back to the main reservoir continuously. You can monitor the main reservoir for pH levels and electroconductivity or nutrient levels instead of testing each plant container separately.

Recirculating or modular deep water culture systems are something you can look into as you gain experience, knowledge, and can better manage a larger, slightly more complex system.

Top-Fed Deep Water Culture

Top-fed and traditional deep water systems are not that different. In both systems, the plant roots hang down towards the reservoir of the solution. With a top-fed system the oxygen-rich solution is pumped up from the reservoir and released directly on the roots of the plant and from there flows back into the reservoir.

The advantage of this over a traditional system is that within the first few weeks of the seedlings' growth the roots are still growing towards the reservoir in traditional systems. This leads to a slower growth rate, whereas a top-fed system allows sooner access to the nutrient solution, which aids in faster growth. Once the roots of the plants reach the reservoir below, both systems are equally matched.

Bubbleponics

The name might sound a little silly, but bubbleponics can be advantageous in the first few weeks of growth. With bubbleponics, you are using a regular deep water culture system, adding a water pump and drip tubes. The water pump will pump the water up to the top of the reservoir where drip tubes will drip feed the young plants until their roots grow down into the reservoir. This top feeding technique that speeds up the growth in young plants, much the same way as a top-fed deep water system does.

What to Grow

Deep water culture systems making use of the raft system can only support lighter plants. Larger plants and top-heavy fruit-bearing plants aren't suitable for this hydroponics system. If you are using a deep water system whereby your plants are in holders fitted into the lid of the container, the plants can be slightly heavier.

Good crops for deep water systems include:

- Bok Choy/Tatsoi
- Lettuce
- Basic
- Okra
- Collard greens
- Kale
- Chard
- Sorrel

Ebb and Flow

Ebb and flow hydroponic systems are also known as flood and drain systems. These systems work by growing plants in a substrate that is in a container above the reservoir. A timer is set, and a water pump pumps the solution into the plant container, flooding it. As the plant container or tray floods, an outlet makes use of gravity to allow the solution to drain back into the reservoir, and this flooding and draining cycle carries on at regular intervals.

Ebb and flow systems are seen as an intermediate hydroponic system that is not only easy and cost-effective to set up but also quite versatile. Ebb and Flow systems may or may not require an air pump to aerate the solution. This depends on how your system is set up.

Advantages of ebb and flow:

- East to set up and cost-effective.
- Easy to use and maintain.
- Sufficient nutrients provided to the plants.

Disadvantages of ebb and flow:

- Malfunction of equipment could leave your plants either high and dry or drowning in the flood phase.
- pH level fluctuations due to the flooding and draining process.
- Potential salt buildup caused by the flood and drain process.

What to Grow

You can grow larger plants and fruit-bearing plants in an ebb and flow system as opposed to a wick or deep water culture system. Some crops that do well in ebb and flow systems include:

- Lettuce
- Tomatoes
- Cucumbers
- Celery
- Watermelon
- Cantaloupe
- Oregano
- Chives

Drip Systems

A drip system is also referred to as a trickle system or a micro-irrigation system. How this works is just as it sounds. A pump will pump nutrient solution through drip tubing and dripping the solutions onto the plants directly. This is not a concept that is unique to hydroponics and has been around for a while as part of traditional soil-based gardening.

Using a drip system allows you to feed your plants slowly, manage water-loss more effectively, and have a greater control over the amount of water and nutrients your plants receive. A drip system consists of a network of tubing and lines and is usually more suitable to larger hydroponic setups, which is often the preferred hydroponic system used by large-scale growers and farming.

The drip system works by either having individual plants in separate pots of substrate or several plants in a tray of growing medium. Each plant has its own dedicated emitter dripping solution onto it. Drip tubing connects the plants to the reservoir and there are two ways to use pressure to supply the solution to the plants. You can use a pump to pump the water or a system that relies on gravity to do the hard work.

The emitters in your system allows you to have full control over the flow of the solution and how much and how quickly your plants are fed. This is what makes a drip system so versatile. You can adjust the levels of flow according to what plants are being irrigated by those specific emitters.

When you use a drip system, the flow needs to be controlled so that the substrate you are using gets an opportunity to breathe in between irrigation sessions. If you leave your drip system unattended and unregulated, you could end up eventually flooding and suffocating your plants. Timers are an essential part of drip systems, for this reason, and you can set specific times of day for the pump to work and shut off to feed your plants in intervals.

A drip system is not an absolute beginner system. It is something to aspire and work your way towards as you gain knowledge and experience, but it takes a lot of planning and careful installation to get it just right. Once you have a drip system set up, running and maintaining it is easy.

Variations

There are two types of drip systems. Recirculating or recovery systems and non-circulating or non-recovery systems. The variation you choose to use comes down to personal choice.

Recirculating/Recovery Drip System

Recirculating drip systems allow the excess nutrient solution that is not absorbed to circulate back into the reservoir. This is popular with smaller home hydroponic setups as it saves water and nutrients. However, there are drawbacks to consider:

- When the run-off nutrient solution is recycled back into the reservoir, it alters the pH balance in the reservoir, which leads to you performing a periodic maintenance on the recirculation system.
- You will have to monitor the pH balance and nutrient concentration of the reservoir regularly to ensure that the correct levels are maintained.

Non-Circulating/Non-Recovery Drip System

A non-circulating drip system operates on the opposite principle to the recirculating variant. This system takes a run-to-waste approach, allowing the excess run-off solution to be collected in a catchment and discarded.

This is not always an effective way of working since it doesn't conserve water or nutrients. However, when using a drip system, run-off is minimal. Non-circulating drip systems are popular with bigger commercial growers who use advanced timing systems to maximize control over their flow and keep wastage to a bare minimum. Not recirculating the waste solution also means that they don't have as much reservoir maintenance to do.

What to Grow

- Pumpkins
- Lettuce
- Onions
- Leeks
- Peas
- Melons
- Radishes

- Tomatoes
- Strawberries
- Cucumbers
- Zucchinis

Nutrient Film Technique

The nutrient film technique (NFT) is a popular and simple hydroponic system that is not entirely different to the ebb and flow system with a different layout. This system is often used to grow plants that are smaller and grow faster.

There are different layouts for a nutrient film hydroponic system, but all of them have certain similarities. All NFT systems are based on a nutrient solution that is kept quite shallow as it pours down through a tube that is typically slanted. The plant roots take the water and nutrients they need as they are exposed to the solution.

Both the ebb and flow system and the nutrient film technique use pumps to bring the nutrient solution to your plants. However, unlike the ebb and flow system, the NTF system does not flood your plants with the solution. Instead, in a nutrient film technique system, the solution is continuously flowing and recirculating through the plant roots.

The NTF system is active, and this means it needs moving parts to run. It isn't passive like a wick system, which works slowly. This is why the nutrient film technique is effective for fast-growing plants.

The design of the NFT system is simple and, if you have the knowledge, not too hard to replicate.

This system consists of two main parts. The channel or the tray in which the plants are grown and the nutrient solution reservoir.

Net pots holding the plants are placed in the channel or grow tray. Each net pot contains a substrate, and the plants are grown in that substrate. As the plants grow, their roots grow downwards to the bottom of the channel where the solution is flowing past. It is also possible to forgo the substrate and just place the plants directly into the net pots after germination and propagation.

A pump has to be employed to pump the water along the channels and past the plant roots. The solution then flows into the drainage system to be recycled back into the reservoir and cycled through the system again.

How this system works is that the channel is positioned at an angle. The pump moves the solution to the highest point of the grow tray. It then flows down to the lowest angle where it is recirculated through a waste or return pipe back into the reservoir. The channel being at an angle negates the need for a secondary pump to help return the excess solution to the reservoir. Gravity does all the work.

As the roots are entirely exposed, they are able to take up enough oxygen, and being partially submerged in a shallow layer of moving nutrient solution lets the plants take up enough water and nutrients.

Advantages of NFT:

- Water and nutrient consumption is relatively low.
- You don't actually have to use growing media.
- It's easy to clean and disinfect the setup.
- Buildup in the root area is prevented due to the continuous flow.
- Water-loss is minimized due to the recirculation of the solution.
- The system is expandable and modular because of its customizable concept.

Disadvantages of NTF:

- If your pump fails to operate due to technical issues or electrical outages, your plants can die very quickly.
- Plants with large taproot systems aren't suitable.
- Plants requiring root support are not suitable.

What to Grow

Various plants can be grown in a nutrient film technique system. The criteria is that they are fast growing and lightweight. Because the roots don't offer much support for the plant, this system is not suitable for larger, heavier plants that need that level of foundation. Some vine plants, such as tomatoes and squash, can be grown in this system using a separate trellis system to support the weight of the fruit as they develop.

Aeroponics

Aeroponics may sound like something futuristic out of a sci-fi novel, but it really isn't. The concept is simple enough, and the system isn't too difficult to build if you have the technical knowledge and experience. However, the truth is that this system is the most complex of the six basic hydroponic systems and is best left alone until you have more knowledge and experience.

An aeroponic system can be made out of a variety of materials, depending on what you have available, your budget, and how you design your system. Many people choose to build their own systems.

An aeroponic system works in an environment where the roots are entirely enclosed. The roots of the plants are continuously or periodically misted with a nutrient-rich solution. The environment is enclosed to prevent moisture loss and aid in minimizing wastage. The plants are partly divided between worlds. Half the plant is above the surface of the reservoir container, allowing it light, oxygen, etc. The root system is below the top of the reservoir, being misted with the solution.

A simple example of an aeroponic system would be if you took a container and cut holes in the top to place net pots to hold the plants. The system inside that enclosed container would allow for misting to occur through spray nozzles. All excess solution would drip back to the bottom of the reservoir container to be recycled and misted again. This is a very simple explanation. The mechanical workings behind it are much more complex, but you get the idea behind it.

Advantages of aeroponics:

- Accelerated plant growth.
- Maintenance of the system is relatively easy once it is set up.
- Lower water and nutrient needs.
- Aeroponic stations are relatively mobile compared to other systems.
- Aeroponic systems are moderately space-saving.

Disadvantages of aeroponics:

- System dependency means that if the system fails, the plant roots will dry out and die.
- Requires technical knowledge and experience.
- The container the plant roots are housed in needs regular cleaning.
- Prohibitive cost.

What to Grow

- Strawberries

- Lettuce
- Basil
- Tomatoes
- Mint
- Leafy greens
- Herbs

Indoor vs Outdoor

The indoor versus outdoor debate is a big question when you enter the world of hydroponics. It is possibly the single most important question to ask yourself before you even begin thinking about what system you want to try working with.

Hydroponics can range from extremely simple to highly complex. It all depends on your own setup, what you can afford, and how much you want to control. For example, in a more complex hydroponic garden, you would house your system indoors or in an enclosed environment, be it a specialized grow room or greenhouse, where you are able to control every aspect from temperature and humidity to light. This kind of setup is quite high-tech, where it requires gadgets and equipment such as heaters, fans, lights, and more to give you that ultimate control. It is also more advanced and best left to those who have the knowledge and experience to maintain and micromanage every aspect of their hydroponic gardens.

For the rest of us, the choice still comes down to indoors or outdoors. If you are going to grow plants indoors, it might be because we live in an apartment, or due to harsh outdoor winter weather, or just personal preference, but you probably aren't going to start out with all the gadgets of advanced indoor hydroponic gardens. There are pros and cons to having your hydroponic system indoors or outdoors. Let's take a look at the good and the bad of both options.

Sunlight: There is no better, or cheaper, source of light for your hydroponic garden than natural sunlight. Sunlight is more readily available from various angles outdoors than indoors. Some systems may even be a challenge or difficult to light properly indoors, whereas they would work well outdoors.

Space: Outdoor hydroponic gardening offers you more space to build your systems. Hydroponics is well known for allowing the growth of more plants in a smaller space than traditional gardening, which makes it ideal for small gardens or indoor gardening if you don't have a garden. However, setting up various systems indoors can be a challenge as far as space is concerned. Some systems may not be suitable for indoor gardening at all.

Affordability: Setting up outdoors means that you can spend the bare minimum on starting out. You aren't going to need extra lights or fans outdoors, whereas indoors you will need to put more thought into lighting and other aspects you may need to augment to grow plants successfully.

Pollination: Running a hydroponic garden indoors may require you to pollinate your plants manually by hand with something like a small paintbrush, whereas an outdoor system is exposed to natural pollinators like bees.

Heat: Controlling temperatures in an outdoor hydroponic system is very difficult and heat affects two aspects of your gardening: the temperature of your nutrient solution and the air temperature around your plants. Plants can take up more water in hotter conditions, which results in an excess of salts and nutrients building up in your substrate or your reservoir that affects the electroconductivity of your solution. To counter this problem, you may need to adjust your nutrient concentration in your solution. Growing plants indoors may afford you more temperature control or stability and the ability to keep temperatures from fluctuating too much.

Growing Seasons: Unlike indoor hydroponics or using a greenhouse, outdoor growing is dictated by the seasons. Therefore, you can only grow what is seasonally suitable and your growing seasons will be shorter. When growing plants indoors with appropriate temperature control, you can grow plants out of season by adding extra light and keeping your system in a warmer environment.

Pests: Pests are more abundant and have free access to your garden when you have your hydroponic system set up outdoors. While this is great for natural pollination, indoor systems have the advantage of being exposed to far fewer garden pests.

Wear and Tear: An outdoor system faces the elements outside all the time and this can lead to additional or faster wear and tear than an indoor system. UV rays from the sun are a big factor in this process.

Control: Setting up outdoors can be a great thing, but you have to relinquish a lot of control that having your hydroponic garden indoors would afford you. Lighting and temperature control aside, things like rainfall can damage your crops by flooding them or weakening your nutrient solution. You need to think carefully about the weather in your area, where you are setting up your system, and how to protect it best from adverse weather conditions when you're growing plants outdoors instead of indoors.

Chapter 4

Step by Step Hydroponic Systems

In this chapter, we're going to guide you through setting up some basic hydroponic gardening systems at home. We're going to cover four of the simpler systems, which are suitable for beginners to take on and try out.

Wick System

The wick system is possibly the easiest hydroponic system to set up and use, which makes it an ideal starting point for newcomers to hydroponic gardening.

For a very basic, single-plant wick system, refer to the passive sub-irrigation section in the previous chapter. For a slightly more complex, multiple-plant wick system, keep reading.

What You Will Need:

- Plants to grow
- Nutrient solution
- A container for your plants to grow in
- A container to act as the reservoir for your nutrient solution
- A suitable growing medium or substrate
- Suitable wick material
- Electric drill

Optional:

- Air pump, airline tube, and air stone
- Black paint

The Reservoir:

One of the simplest ways to create a reservoir is to use a rectangular tub with a lid. Using a container with a lid means that you can rest the grow tray on top of the lid. A lid will also help keep debris out of the nutrient solution and, if you're using a tub of a solid color, the light will be blocked out and prevent the growth of algae. If you are using a clear or translucent white container, you may need to paint it black to prevent light reaching the nutrient solution.

The Grow Tray:

For the grow tray, you can use another tub of the same size as the one you are using for the reservoir. However, it may be a good idea to use a shallower container if your reservoir tub is taller to let your plants see more of the world and to allow you to admire them. Ensure that your grow tray is compatible with your reservoir and that it fits comfortably and won't slide or fall off.

The Wicks:

As the wicks need to transfer water from the reservoir to the grow tray, they need to be made of a material that absorbs liquid well but won't easily rot from being wet all the time. Wicks can successfully be made from a variety of materials, including:

- Tiki torch wicks
- Strands from a mop head
- Felt strips
- Cotton rope
- Wool strips or wool rope

Air Pump:

Using an air pump in a wick system is optional. Because you are growing your plants in a growing medium, this should provide air pockets that allow your plants to take up oxygen. However, providing an oxygenated nutrient solution is always a good idea. You can purchase an aquatic air pump and air stone from a pet store.

Instructions:

1. Fill your reservoir with nutrient solution. Leave approximately a one-inch gap between the top of the solution and the lid.
2. If you are using an air pump and air stone, drill a hole in the side of your reservoir tub near the top, above the waterline, to thread the pump tube through. Once you have threaded the tube through the hole, attach your air stone and lay it at the bottom of the reservoir.
3. Drill holes into the lid of the reservoir and the bottom of the grow tray and make sure they line up. Your wicks will pass through these holes into both containers.

4. Thread your wicks through the holes in both the reservoir lid and bottom of the grow tray. Make sure that your wicks are long enough to sit comfortably in your grow medium and in the nutrient solution so that as the nutrient solution level drops the wick will be long enough to keep in contact.
5. It is a handy idea to glue your grow tray to the lid of your reservoir to create a single unit from the tray and the lid. After, seal the edges of the wick holes with silicone to prevent leaks.
6. Add your grow medium to your grow tray and plant your plants in the grow tray. Make sure to leave enough space around and between plants for them to grow to their full size.

That's it; your hydroponic wick system is done.

Deep Water Culture System

Deep Water Culture is another starter system suitable for beginners in hydroponics. These reservoirs can be made from various things, including larger containers such as buckets, tubs, or tanks, to small containers like glass jars. The type of reservoir used is dependent on the plants being grown, space available, and the preference of the gardener.

What You Will Need:

- Plants to grow
- Nutrient solution
- A container to act as the reservoir for your nutrient solution
- Net plant cups/pots
- A suitable grow medium with a decent wicking ability
- Craft knife
- Pencil
- Electric drill
- Air pump, airline tube, and air stone
- Black paint (optional)

The Reservoir:

You can use a bucket or tall tub with a lid. If you are using a clear or translucent white container for your reservoir, you may need to paint it black to prevent light from reaching the nutrient solution and thus allowing algae to grow. Using a solid-color container is helpful if you don't want to muck around with painting your reservoir.

The Grow Tray:

Unlike the wick system which has a separate grow tray, the lid of your reservoir will become your grow tray. When you are creating your deep water culture system, keep in mind the number of plants you want to grow and budget enough space around and between the plant cups for the plants to reach their full size comfortably without overcrowding.

The Air Pump:

You can purchase an air pump, air stone, and airline tube from a pet store that sells aquatic supplies. An air pump is an essential part of your deep water culture system. This is going to be a sealed system so air cannot get into your plant roots, which will make aeration of your nutrient solution important for your plants' survival.

Instructions:

1. Position the plant cups in the lid of your container according to where you are going to place them and draw a stencil around the base of the cups on the lid.
2. Using a craft knife, cut out the holes for the plant cups. You may need to adjust the size of the holes until your plant cups fit snuggly but do not fall through.
3. Fill your reservoir with nutrient solution until the solution touches the base of the plant cups. While your plants are young and in the first stages of growing, their roots will not yet have grown down into the solution. Your wicking growing medium needs to be in contact with the solution to be able to transfer it upward to the plant until it has grown enough for the roots to hang down into the solution.
4. Drill a hole in the side of your reservoir at the top and feed your airline tube through that hole. Connect either end to the air pump and air stone and place the air stone at the bottom of the reservoir.
5. Fit the lid securely onto the reservoir, fill the plant cups with your grow medium, and plant your plants into the cups.

When using a deep water culture system with a fixed lid, it is imperative that your solution level does not drop below a level where the plant roots can reach it. To prevent this from happening when you are not around to monitor the solution level, you can either use a Mariotte's bottle or a float valve, often called a ballcock, attached to a refilling system.

When it comes time to change your nutrient solution, you can use an electrical conductivity meter to test the nutrient level. Testing the electroconductivity of the solution just means testing the strength of the solution or nutrient concentration. You use the meter to test the solution and adjust it accordingly. Alternatively, you can change it out completely on a set schedule, for instance, once a week.

Variation:

Another way of preventing the solution level from dropping too low for the plant roots to reach it is to use a floating system instead of a suspension. A floating system makes use of a raft-like way of suspending your plants on the surface of the water. You can use heavy buoyant plastic or something like Styrofoam or create a raft in whichever way that suits you. Your plants will then float on the liquid's surface and drop with the solution level, which will ensure that the roots are always in contact with the solution.

Ebb and Flow System

An ebb and flow, or flood and drain, hydroponic system is a little bit more complicated to build than a wick or deep water culture system. However, it's still suitable and achievable for those starting out.

What You Will Need:

- Plants to grow
- Nutrient solution
- A container to act as the reservoir for your nutrient solution
- A container to act as your grow tray
- A suitable grow medium
- Electric drill
- Inlet and outlet fittings or an ebb and flow fittings kit
- Submersible pump and tubing
- Analog or digital timer
- Air pump, airline tube, and air stone (optional)
- Black paint (optional)

The Reservoir:

For an ebb and flow system, a larger reservoir means that you won't have to refill it as often. Use a tall rectangular tub with a lid— a solid color works best to keep light from getting to your nutrient solution. Alternatively, you can paint a clear or translucent-white tub black.

The Grow Tray:

Use a tub with a similar base surface area as your reservoir tub, but that is shallower in height. Your grow tray doesn't need to have a lid.

Inlet and Outlet Fittings:

If you are more of a crafty, DIY person, you can go down to your local hardware store, explain your plans, and ask for advice on which fittings will best suit your needs. Alternatively, to make your life a little easier, you can purchase an ebb and flow fittings kit from a nursery or online hydroponics store.

The Submersible Pump:

You can find a submersible pump at either a nursery or some hardware stores. This is the same kind of pump used in garden water features. It doesn't need to be the biggest or best model on the market. Speak to the consultant at the store you are buying it from for advice on the correct size for your needs.

The Air Pump:

For an ebb and flow system, an air pump is optional. Your plants will be growing in a growing medium, which should provide oxygen through air pockets between the substrate particles. However, more oxygen is never a bad thing when it comes to growing big, healthy plants.

The Timer:

You can use either an analog or a digital timer, as long as it works in a 24-hour rotation. An idea is to buy a swimming pool pump timer that people use to automate their pool cleaning systems at home.

Instructions:

1. Glue the base of your grow tray to the top of the lid of your reservoir.
2. Drill holes through the lid-base combination for the inlet on one side and the outlet on the other.
3. Fit your inlet and outlet fittings to each hole and make sure they are snug and won't leak. If necessary, you can use silicone to seal them off properly.
4. Drill a hole in the side of the reservoir, near the top, above the waterline of your solution and thread the wires for the submersible pump through the hole to the

outside of the reservoir. Place the pump at the bottom of the reservoir and seal the wires in place with silicone at the hole.
5. If you are using an air pump, drill another hole at the same height a couple of inches apart from the submersible pump's wire hole. Thread your airline tube through the hole and attach the air pump on the outside of the reservoir and the air stone on the inside at the bottom of the reservoir.
6. Connect the timer to the submersible pump and test it to ensure that it works correctly.
7. Fill your reservoir with nutrient solution and ensure that the level of the solution is a couple of inches below the holes for the air pump and submersible pump.
8. Place your growing medium in your grow tray and plant your plants in the medium.
9. Place the grow tray/lid of the reservoir container on the reservoir snuggly.
10. Set your timer to activate the pump at the required regular intervals and you're done.

Nutrient Film Technique

A nutrient film technique system isn't difficult to set up. It just takes some time and planning and a little bit of space.

What You Will Need:

- Plants to grow.
- Nutrient solution.
- A container to act as the reservoir for your nutrient solution.
- Tubing or pipes to act as your grow tray
- Net plant pots/cups
- Electric drill
- Pencil
- Tubing to carry the solution from the reservoir to the grow tray channel
- Submersible pump
- Black paint (optional)
- Piping to drain the excess solution into the reservoir (optional)

The Reservoir:

The reservoir can be made from almost anything you like, from a bucket to a five-gallon drum. The choice is up to you. It is recommended to use a container of a solid color or to paint it black to prevent algae growth due to sunlight exposure of your nutrient solution.

The Grow Tray:

Unlike with other hydroponic systems, the nutrient film technique uses channels to grow the plants in. Most DIY systems make use of PVC pipes or tubes. This is so that it is more easily placed at an angle to reduce the inner surface area the nutrient solution travels along. This provides a narrow exit point for the solution so that it flows directly back into the reservoir without spilling.

The Submersible Pump:

Submersible pumps are available at hardware stores and nurseries. You are going to use the same type of pump used in water features for gardens. This does not need to be a large pump. Speak to a store consultant to help decide on the correct size pump for your needs. The rate of flow of your nutrient solution through the channel should be approximately ¼ to ½ gallon per minute. The strength of your pump needs to be able to maintain that flow rate and should be taken into consideration when you're purchasing the pump.

Instructions:

Before you start constructing your nutrient film technique system, you need to consider where you are going to set it up and what you are going to use as a frame to support the system. The grow tray channel needs to be set up at a slope of approximately 1:30 to 1:40. What this means is that for every 30 to 40 inches of the channel, the lower end needs to be dropped by one inch to create the slope. Here's an example: If you use a 40-inch long channel, the end that the solution flows out of will be one inch lower than the end the solution is pumped into. You also need to ensure that the channel stays straight all the way through. Any sagging will cause the solution to pool. Therefore, depending on the length of your channel, you may need to add additional support in sections that may sag over time.

1. Place your submersible pump into your reservoir container and measure the length of tube you will need to connect the pump to the mouth of your grow channel. When you have the right length, secure the tube to the mouth of the channel, and fill the reservoir with nutrient solution.

2. Determine the spacing of your plants and using the plant cups as stencils. Draw outlines along the top length of your grow channel. Keep in mind the space plants will need between each other to prevent overcrowding as they grow to their full size.
3. Cut or drill holes along the top of the grow channel for your plant cups and place the cups in the holes.
4. Set your channel up according to the correctly calculated slope with the lower end of the channel directly over the reservoir. It can even be touching the rim of the container. The closer the end of your channel is to the top of the reservoir, the less splashing will occur which minimizes any possible mess.
5. Place your plants in the cups and switch your pump on. You may or may not want to use a growing medium in the cups.
6. The pump should be pumping nutrient solution from the reservoir to the top end of the channel. The solution should be flowing through the channel, making contact with the plant roots, and exiting the channel through the other end to return to the reservoir.

What you should keep in mind for this setup is that in this particular, simple design the reservoir is not covered, which allows debris and light to reach your nutrient solution. Additional steps to take to create a more enclosed system include:

- Use a reservoir container with a lid.
- Attach an elbow-shaped piece of tube or pipe to the exit end of your grow tube with a straight piece of tube that will feed directly back into your reservoir.
- Drill a hole in the reservoir lid to feed the water pump pipe through to the mouth of your grow tube and cut a hole in the lid to accommodate the downpipe from your grow tube.

Chapter 5

Hydroponic Gardening: Nutrients

Every plant needs nutrients to survive. Traditionally, soil-based gardening plants draw their nutrients from the soil and to boost their health and growth gardeners would add manure, compost, and chemical fertilizers. However, hydroponics works differently. Without the use of soil, we need to provide the plants with all their nutrients through the solution we feed them.

Macro and Micro

There are two main categories that nutrients can be divided into. Macronutrients and micronutrients. Macronutrients are those nutrients a plant needs in large quantities. Examples of plant macronutrients include hydrogen, oxygen, potassium, and phosphorus. Micronutrients are those nutrients a plant needs only small quantities of, but they are still vital to the plant's health. Examples of plant micronutrients include copper, zinc, and iron.

If plants do not get their required amount of each nutrient, be it a macronutrient or a micronutrient, they are not able to grow and develop properly and they may not flower and bear fruit or vegetables.

PH Balance

An important factor to consider in addition to nutrients is the pH balance of your nutrient solution. This can determine the amount of nutrients your plant can absorb from the solution and thus has a big impact on its health. Your nutrient solution should be tested regularly to monitor the pH balance and adjust the solution accordingly. To adjust your pH levels, you can use a commercially bought agent that will offer a pH butter to adjust the balance for you.

Not All Plants Are Equal

Just like people, plants are different and different types of plants will require different nutrient concentrations and pH levels to support optimum health and growth. You will need to research each of the types of plants you want to grow and what their individual needs are so that you can correctly mix your nutrient solution and adjust the pH balance to suit each plant.

Temperature

When you are running an indoor hydroponic system, fluctuations in temperature, weather, and seasons aren't a big concern. When your hydroponic garden is outside, you need to consider these environmental variables.

Your nutrient solution should be kept at a consistent temperature, ideally room temperature. Room temperature is considered to be between 70 and 78 degrees Fahrenheit. If your setup is outside, you may need to consider purchasing water heaters, like the ones used in fish tanks, to keep your solution from getting too cold. During the summer months, you should be mindful to keep your reservoirs in the shade and, if necessary, use cool water when you top them up.

Buy Commercial or Make Your Own

This is a debate that can rage on for ages. Everybody has a different opinion on whether to mix your own nutrient solution at home or purchase commercially made concentration.

When buying commercial concentrations that are pre-mixed, you often buy two bottles: a bottle of macronutrients and a bottle of micronutrients. They are purchased separately because not all the ingredients, in their concentrated forms, play well with each other when thrown together in the same bottle. Some commercial nutrient packs come with several parts to offer you more control over the specific nutrient levels in your solution according to the growth phase your plants are going through.

Mixing your own nutrient solution can be tricky and requires knowledge and experience. It's not impossible, but it is very easy to get it wrong, to the detriment of your plants.

If you are new to hydroponics, you should consider starting off buying commercial nutrient concentrations. You can take your time to learn how to go about mixing your own solution at home and try your hand at it when you have more experience and knowledge.

Nutrient Ingredients

All commercially bought nutrient solutions should contain all the minerals and elements necessary for plant health.

- Potassium (K)
- Nitrogen (N)
- Calcium (Ca)
- Phosphorous (P)
- Sulphur (S)
- Magnesium (Mg)
- Iron (Fe)
- Copper (Cu)
- Manganese (Mn)
- Boron (B)
- Zinc (Zn)
- Chlorine (Cl)
- Molybdate (Mo)

Different manufacturers may vary in the exact concentration of each of these elements in their nutrient products, as there is no consensus on precise levels required. Don't worry too much about the precise concentrations but rather ensure that all of them are in the product or package you are purchasing. Some manufacturers may also include nonessential ingredients such as cobalt (Co) and silica (Si). While these additional ingredients are not life-sustaining for your plants, they can be beneficial in their growth.

Nutrient Deficiency

There are many reasons plants may become deficient in certain nutrients. These range from internal factors and climate to miscalculation of nutrients or solution strength. Let's look at what happens to your plants when they have certain deficiencies.

Nitrogen: Short plants, pale greenish-yellow leaves, and purple discoloration on the underside of tomato plant stems and leaves.

Phosphorous: Stunted growth, dark green foliage, older leaves become symptomatic first. There is a delay in plant maturation, and some plants develop a deficiency when uptake is prohibited by cold conditions as opposed to nutrient solution issues.

Potassium: Yellowed older leaves with scattered brown or black spots and the foliage tissue dies. Severely deficient plants will exhibit stunted growth and all foliage will be affected and curl.

Sulfur: While sulfur deficiency is uncommon, new foliage will become symptomatic first, displaying yellowed leaves.

Magnesium: Common in tomato plants. Leaf veins remain green with yellow areas between them.

Calcium: New foliage becomes symptomatic first with smaller, distorted leaves displaying dead spots. Root tips may die, and buds don't develop.

Iron: In contrast with magnesium deficiency, younger foliage is affected first, displaying green leaf veins with yellowing in between them.

Chlorine: Leaves wilt, are yellow, and die. These plants have stunted root growth with a thickening at the ends.

Manganese: Yellowing of the leaves between the veins, browning, and then dropping of leaves.

Boron: Smaller plant size with potential dying of growth points, ends of roots swell and discolor, eventually the plant will display brittle, thickened leaves with potential yellow spotting and curling.

Zinc: Plants are shorter, reduced length between nodes, smaller leaves that may have puckered or odd edges and potentially yellowing between the veins of the leaves.

Copper: Whilst rare, copper deficiency leads to dark green new leaves that are deformed and may have dry, brown spots.

Molybdenum: Yellowing between the veins in older foliage, which continues to newer foliage. The edges of leaves may appear scorched.

Nutrient Solution: Balance and Concentration

Nutrient solutions are about more than just getting the quantity of all the specific nutrients correct to suit a particular type of plant. It is just as important to get the concentration of the nutrients within your solution correct. You can use an electroconductivity meter to measure the concentration of your solution and match that reading to what is appropriate for your particular plants. Just as with pH and nutrient balances, you will have to research your plants and find out what each plant's ideal EC reading is.

If your EC is too high, plant growth is stunted, and your plants will lose water back into the over-concentrated nutrient solution around the roots. This usually shows itself as shorter plants with smaller leaves and a darker green color. The opposite will happen if your EC is too low; plants may take on too much water and will appear limp.

Chapter 6

Diseases, Pests, Common Problems

Hydroponic gardening offers a variety of advantages over traditional soil-based gardening, but that doesn't mean it doesn't have its fair share of problems. Growing hydroponically indoors or in an enclosed environment such as a greenhouse does offer you a lot more control over setting up your hydroponic system outdoors. However, there are common issues that every hydroponic system is likely to face.

Common Problems

Water + Nutrients + Light = Algae

It's no secret that algae in your nutrient solution reservoir can be problematic. Whenever the three components that facilitate algae growth come together, namely nutrients, water, and light, it will develop. Algae is bad for your hydroponic system because with algae comes fungus gnats and when fungus gnats arrive, they will damage your plant roots.

The Fix

Prevent algae growth by making not only your reservoir but as much of your whole system as lightproof as possible. Use solid colored materials where possible. If you can't lay your hands on solid-colored materials, try painting them to block out the light. Ensure that your plant holes in your system are only big enough to fit the plant cups or pots. Any that aren't being used should be covered with a solid material that will keep light out.

Leaks

Because hydroponic systems work with a water-based nutrient solution, they can be prone to leaks developing within the system. Leaks happen for a wide range of reasons from wear and tear, to the system being clogged, and power outages that stop pumps from working.

The Fix

Check your system regularly. This will help you pick up leaks from wear and tear before they become a bigger problem. Check your drip emitters, valves, even your plant roots. You will quickly notice if a potential part of your system that has become clogged is threatening to overthrow your hydroponic garden into leakages and flooding. Make sure that your reservoir can safely hold the entire volume of the nutrient solution circulating in your system so that if a pump breaks or stops working without electricity, the reservoir won't overflow, such as with a nutrient film technique. If you are worried about the threat a power outage could pose to your plants themselves, invest in a backup power system that is battery operated and will kick in if the power goes out.

Nutrient Deficiencies, pH, EC

A nutrient imbalance can negatively affect your pH and electroconductivity and this can occur through no fault of your own. Aside from grower error, environmental conditions can affect the uptake of nutrients and water in plants.

The Fix

Firstly, research each type of plant thoroughly and make notes of its nutrient requirements, pH preference, and ideal EC so that you can monitor the solution correctly. Temperature control and testing your nutrient solution regularly will help you monitor your solution and adjust it to keep it at the optimum level for your plants.

Hard Water

Using hard water in your hydroponic gardening system can lead to nutrient deficiencies in your plants without you realizing it. Make sure the water you are using contains no more than 200 parts per million (ppm) total dissolved solids by using a total dissolved solids (TDS) meter. The issue is that tap water has added chemicals and dissolved solids that aren't able to be absorbed by your plants and can cause your plants to be unable to take up sufficient nutrients from the solution.

The Fix

Test your water with a TDS meter to ensure it is below 200 ppm. If you are having issues with hard water, you can use an inexpensive activated coal filter to reduce the amount of dissolved solids in the water. A more expensive option is a reverse osmosis filter, which removes almost all dissolved solids.

Heat and Humidity

Heat can cause your plants to suck up more water from your solution, resulting in a nutrient concentration that is too high. This, in turn, causes salt buildup and toxicity. Low humidity can cause plants to transpire more and lose valuable moisture from their foliage faster than they can absorb it, leading to leaf burn. High humidity can cause plants to be unable to transpire efficiently, leading to a buildup of fluids in the foliage, blossom end rot, and tip burn. High humidity also prevents the plant from moving adequate calcium up to the developing parts of the plant where it is needed, which will mimic the appearance of calcium deficiency.

The Fix

If your hydroponic system is outdoors, you can try to protect your plants from the heat by installing shade netting to provide more shade. For humidity issues, increase the ventilation and airflow both outdoors and indoors, garden fans could be an addition outdoors while regular fans and opening as many windows as possible could help indoors. If you can monitor the humidity, it should ideally be around 70–75% for most plants. If you are having low humidity problems in a grow room or greenhouse, you can try using a humidifier to increase the humidity to a more suitable level for your plants.

Plant Diseases

Just as people get sick, plants can fall ill as well. Being vigilant, checking your plant health regularly, knowing what to look for, and how to treat it can safeguard your hydroponic garden from disease.

Hydroponic gardens allow you to grow your plants closer together. They also feed off the same nutrient solution. This creates the ideal environment for disease to spread among your plants like wildfire and devastate whole gardens.

Common Diseases

Downy Mildew: Appears predominantly on the underside of leaves, does not appear powdery and is not to be confused with powdery mildew.

Powdery Mildew: Appears as a white powder sprinkled over stems and leaves.

Gray Mold: First appears as spots on leaves, progressing to fuzzy patches, which spread until the entire plant is musty and brown in color.

Root Rot: Appears as yellow, wilted plants with pulpy roots. This is caused by too many water microorganisms.

Pythium: An organism that seems like a fungus, lethal and extremely infectious.

The Solution

Clean Clothes: Diseases can hitch a lift to your indoor and outdoor hydroponic garden on your clothes. If you have been out and about, change clothes before working around your system.

Clean Up: Excess water and humidity are big culprits for the onset of mildew or mold diseases. Clean up any excess water, leaks, spills, etc. Lower the humidity by increasing airflow.

Clean Plants: Remove decaying plant matter or prune plants of any diseased foliage. Check for decay, rot in roots, and remove them immediately. Change your solution regularly to prevent the spread of disease through the recirculating solution.

These simple steps will help prevent the onset and spread of plant diseases in your hydroponic garden.

Plant Pests

Pests do not just plague traditional gardens; they also affect hydroponic plants. To ward off the enemy, you need to know what it looks like first.

Common Pests

Spider Mites: Tiny, less than 1mm in size, and may go unnoticed until the infestation is large. Check plants for webbing similar to spider webs and gently wipe the undersides of leaves with a clean tissue. Spider mite blood streaks indicate they are present.

Aphids: Green, grey, or black in appearance. They tend to congregate around stems, sucking the plant sap and weakening the plant.

Thrips: Small in size, approximately 5mm, and suck leaves dry. It can be difficult to identify, keep an eye out for little black, metallic-looking specks on the tops of leaves progressing to leaves browning and drying.

Fungus Gnats: Adult gnats are harmless, but larvae do serious damage. Larvae damage roots, stunting plant growth, and has a potential to cause bacterial infection.

Whiteflies: Tiny, approximately 1mm, moth-like appearance. Easy to see but hard to get rid of because they fly. White spots and yellowing are caused by sucking the plants dry.

Mealy Bugs: Mealy bugs are white, fluffy in appearance, and hard to get rid of because of the hard outer shell. They suck sap from plant stems.

The Solution

Beneficial Bugs: Some beneficial predatory bugs such as ladybirds and nematodes can help rid your garden of harmful pests. Ladybugs feast on aphids, for instance.

Sprays: Opt for non-harmful sprays that can be used as a deterrent or treat invasions. Avoid poisons made with harsh chemicals.

Sticky Traps: Sticky traps, similar to flypaper, will trap pests before they can get to your plants or help reduce an invasion. Yellow sticky cards draw whiteflies and fungus gnats. Blue sticky cards lure thrips.

Vigilance: Being vigilant and checking your plants regularly will help discourage an infestation from getting out of hand, especially with hard to remove pests like mealy bugs. The younger bugs can be treated with chemicals before the outer shell hardens. Adult bugs need to be removed individually using alcohol and a cotton bud.

Chapter 7

Tips and Myths

Who doesn't love handy tips that make your life easier, provide you with ideas, and help you get the most out of what you're doing? In this section, we will provide you with useful tips to aid you in growing a successful hydroponic garden.

Tips for Hydroponic Gardening

Plant Selection

Not all hydroponic systems can support the same plants. It is important to select your plants according to the system you are using and how much space you have. Your choice in a hydroponic system will be determined by the space you have available to set the system up and where you are setting it up.

Start Simple

Big, beautiful hydroponic systems may look impressive and you may be aspiring to have a stunning garden. However, hydroponic gardening is all about taking it one step at a time. Start with a smaller, simpler system and grow plants that are easy to look after and grow. As you gain experience, knowledge, and confidence, you can expand and build up to bigger, better things. Hardy herbs are an excellent choice to start with. If you are unsure, ask your local nursery for their suggestions of which plants to start with in your hydroponic garden.

Growing Season Guide

As you grow your plants, observe and take note of the changes they undergo at different phases of growth and how long these phases last. This will help you compile a guide for future growing seasons.

pH and Deficiencies

When you notice a deficiency in your plants, make testing and adjusting your pH balance your first call to action to fix the problem. Many deficiency issues can easily be solved by fixing your pH because an incorrect pH can lead to plants being unable to take up the necessary nutrients effectively.

The Root of a Problem

Regularly check the roots of your plants. The roots are the most important aspect of your plant health. Without properly functioning roots, the plant cannot acquire the correct nutrients and oxygen for optimal growth. Check for damage, pests, infection, etc. to maintain a healthy root system and thus a healthy plant.

Light Up Their Life

Light is an important source of energy for plants. Without light, they cannot photosynthesize and cannot grow. If you are growing your hydroponic garden outdoors, consider the needs of the plants you are growing. Do they need full sun, partial sun, afternoon shade, or full shade? Once you know the light requirements, you can determine where best to position your system for the best light exposure. If you are growing your garden indoors, consider how much natural light the room gets. If there is not enough light to meet the plants' needs, you may consider employing additional lighting to help give them enough light.

Outdoor Elements

Outdoor hydroponic gardens that are not in a greenhouse will be subject to the elements. You may need to find ways to help shelter your plants from the heat, cold, wind, etc. such as using shade netting for shade or as a windbreak, using garden fans, and other ways to help protect them.

Temperature

When you are growing your plants indoors or in a greenhouse, try to keep the temperature as constant at the optimal temperature for your choice of plants. This will help them grow better and faster, and if you are going to grow all year round, trick your plants into thinking that all year is growing season. Keeping your nutrient solution at a constant temperature will also help convince the plants that there is no such thing as winter or being 'out of season'.

System Cleaning

You should be cleaning your hydroponic system regularly to help ward off contamination, which can lead to unhealthy plants. You should aim to clean your reservoir every two to three weeks. Clean any solid residue build-up in tubes and on the reservoir walls. Clean out the grow trays between every growing season if you are growing plants like lettuce which require new plants to grow every grow season. To clean your reservoir or system parts, use a 10% bleach solution and rinse thoroughly afterward.

Hydroponic Myths Busted!

Hydroponics is shrouded in its fair share of myths and misconceptions. Let's bust some of the most common myths about growing a hydroponic garden.

It's Unnatural

This couldn't be further from the truth. Plants grown in a hydroponic system need the same nutrients, oxygen, and environmental factors to grow and be healthy. All you are doing is removing the soil component of traditional gardening and feeding your plants the nutrients directly mixed with their water. You are not adding any harmful or artificial hormones or chemicals to your nutrient solutions.

Difficult and Complicated

As you have realized by reading this book, hydroponic gardening doesn't have to be rocket science. You can make your system as simple or as complicated as you want it to be, and that will all depend on your knowledge and experience level.

No Pesticides Necessary

As much as it would be amazing for this to be true, it's not the case. While soil-borne pests and diseases are eliminated from your worries, even indoor or greenhouse systems still fall prey to some pesky problems. Be vigilant and use as many natural or less harmful methods of prevention or cure as you can before resorting to more potent chemical warfare on bugs and illness.

It's Only Indoors

While you may have seen hydroponics being employed on a farming scale in large tunnels and greenhouses, it's available for everyone to try. Hydroponics in a controlled, enclosed environment may produce bigger, better yields, but that's not to say you can't successfully grow healthy plants for harvest outdoors.

Harmful Lighting

Stemming from the harmful lights of tanning beds, there is a misconception that grow lights used in hydroponics are harmful to you. These lights do not give off enough UV light to be harmful, just enough to grow plants when natural sunlight isn't sufficient.

Conclusion

As you can see from reading this book, hydroponics is easy. It's accessible to anyone, and it works. It's no more difficult than traditional soil-based gardening and anyone can do it — even kids. There are systems to cater to every growing need and different complexities to suit different experience levels from complete beginners to experienced growers. Some of the systems are more expensive to invest in, while others are much more budget-friendly. Some of these systems you can even make by upcycling old materials, recycling recyclable materials you would normally throw away, or make them from bits and pieces you may have lying around. Other basic systems need a few more resources that you will need to buy, but won't break the bank to build them.

Hydroponics is your key to soilless urban gardening in small spaces, with little or no garden, and with a small budget. You can decide how small or big you want to go, how basic or complex. The possibilities are endless. The only limit is your creativity. You can grow delicious fruits, herbs, and vegetables in your own home or garden. All you need to do is set up the most suitable hydroponics system for your space and start growing. It really is as easy as that. The best part about hydroponics is that it saves precious water and you can grow your favorites all year long in the right environment. You won't have to worry about fruits and veggies only being available in certain seasons.

So, what are you waiting for? You're armed with all the knowledge you need. Now it's time to go and build your own hydroponic system and start growing!

References

5 Gallon Bucket DWC System. (n.d). Home Hydro System. http://www.homehydrosystems.com/system_plans/Water%20culture%20systems/5-gallon-DWC-system/5-gallon-DWC-system.html

9 Tips for Beginners Creating a Hydroponic System. (2019, May 25). Origin Hydroponics. https://originhydroponics.com/hydroponics-tips/

10 Most Common Hydroponics Pests & Diseases and How to Fight Them! (2017, May 26). Advanced Nutrients. https://www.advancednutrients.com/articles/hydroponics-plants-pests-and-diseases/

10 Myths of Hydroponics. (2011, February 11). Cocoponics. http://www.cocoponics.co/hydroponics/10-myths-of-hydroponics

15 Common Problems with Hydroponics (and How to Fix Them). (n.d.). Smart Garden Guide. https://smartgardenguide.com/problems-with-hydroponics/

20 Advantages & Disadvantages of Hydroponics That You Should Know. (2019, August 6). Green and Vibrant. https://www.greenandvibrant.com/advantages-disadvantages-of-hydroponics

Aeroponics – Benefits and Disadvantages. (n.d.). Gardening Site https://www.gardeningsite.com/aeroponics/aeroponics-benefits-and-disadvantages/

Aeroponic System. (n.d). Home Hydro Systems. http://www.homehydrosystems.com/hydroponic-systems/aeroponics_systems.html

Basic Hydroponic Systems and How They Work. (n.d.). Simply Hydroponics. https://www.simplyhydro.com/system/

Cartwright, M. (2018, July 27). *Hanging Gardens of Babylon*. Ancient History Encyclopedia. https://www.ancient.eu/Hanging_Gardens_of_Babylon/

Commonly Found Pests and Diseases in Hydro Plants. (2017, August 1). Hydroponic Store. https://thehydroponicsstore.com/grow-blog/commonly-found-pests-and-diseases-in-hydro-plants/

Considering Common Hydroponic System Problems. (n.d.). Jason's Indoor Guide. https://www.jasons-indoor-guide-to-organic-and-hydroponics-gardening.com/hydroponic-system.html

D'Anna, C. (2019, July 22). *Ebb and Flow Systems of Hydroponic Gardens.* The Spruce. https://www.thespruce.com/hydroponic-gardens-ebb-and-flow-systems-1939219

D'Anna, C. (2019, October 14). *Hydroponic Nutrient Solution Basics.* The Spruce. https://www.thespruce.com/hydroponic-nutrient-solution-basics-1939228

Deep Water Culture (DWC) - The Definitive Guide. (n.d.). Hydro Gardeners Lab. https://hydrogardenerslab.com/deep-water-culture-guide/

Dwc Hydroponics System – The Ultimate Guide. (n.d.). Gardening Heavn. https://gardeningheavn.com/dwc-hydroponics/

Ebb & Flow (Flood and Drain) Hydroponic System. (2019, January 6). Green and Vibrant. https://www.greenandvibrant.com/ebb-and-flow-hydroponics

Espiritu, K. (2019, October 3). *History of Hydroponics: When Was Hydroponics Invented?* Epic Gardening. https://www.epicgardening.com/history-of-hydroponics/

Espiritu, K. (2019, October 3). *Hydroponics vs Soil: 7 Reasons Hydroponics Wins.* Epic Gardening. https://www.epicgardening.com/hydroponics-vs-soil/

Espiritu, K. (2019, November 30). The Nutrient Film Technique Explained. Epic Gardening. https://www.epicgardening.com/nutrient-film-technique/#Benefits_of_NFT

Fogarty, R. (2010, November 14). *Hydroponics – Static Solution Culture Technique.* https://ezinearticles.com/?Hydroponics---Static-Solution-Culture-Technique&id=5381873

Foust, Z. (2019, June 26). *Recirculating vs. Drain-to-Waste Hydroponic Systems.* Crop King. https://www.cropking.com/blog/recirculating-vs-drain-waste-hydroponic-systems

Gibs, E. (2017, August 28). *Busting Hydroponic Myths.* http://placecallhome.com/healthy-home/busting-hydroponics-myths/#Hydroponics_affect_the_environment

Grow It Best. (2019, May 23). *Hydroponic Gardening System: Tips and Tricks for Growing Plants in Hydroponic Systems.* Medium. https://medium.com/@growitbest/hydroponic-gardening-system-tips-and-tricks-for-growing-plants-in-hydroponic-systems-47c7e804a3d2

Growing Mediums and Hydroponics. (n.d). Home Hydro System. http://www.homehydrosystems.com/mediums/mediums_page.html#List_of_different_types_of_growing_media

How to Germinate Hydroponic Seedlings. (2018, December 30). PowerHouse Hydroponics. https://www.powerhousehydroponics.com/how-to-germinate-hydroponic-seedlings/

Hydroponics. (2020, April 7). In Wikipedia. https://en.wikipedia.org/wiki/Hydroponics

Hydroponics: Advantages and Disadvantages. (n.d). Dyna-Gro. https://dyna-gro.com/hydroponics-advantages-and-disadvantages/

Hydroponic Drip System Explained. (2019, January 6). Green and Vibrant. https://www.greenandvibrant.com/hydroponic-drip-system

Hydroponics Myths. (2014, March 24). Advanced Nutrients. https://www.advancednutrients.com/articles/hydroponics-myths/

Hydroponic Soda Bottle System. (n.d.). Instructables. https://www.instructables.com/id/Hydroponic-Soda-Bottle-System/

Hydroponic Wick Systems: The Training Wheels of the Hydroponic World. (2019, January 6). Green and Vibrant. https://www.greenandvibrant.com/hydroponic-wick-systems

Hydroponic Wick System – The Ultimate Guide. Gardening Heavn. https://gardeningheavn.com/hydroponic-wick-system/

Kilpinen, J. (n.d). *How to Build Your Own Flood and Drain (Ebb and Flow) System.* Just 4 Growers. http://www.just4growers.com/stream/hydroponic-growing-techniques/how-to-build-your-own-flood-and-drain-(ebb-and-flow)-system.aspx

Morgan, L. (n.d). *Nutrients – Under and Over Use.* Simply Hydroponics. https://www.simplyhydro.com/nutrients/

Morgan, L. (2020, March 6). *What's the Problem? Hydroponic Troubleshooting.* Simply Hydroponics. https://www.maximumyield.com/whats-the-problem-hydroponic-troubleshooting/2/1232

N.F.T. (Nutrient Film Technique) Systems. (n.d.). Home Hydro System. http://www.homehydrosystems.com/hydroponic-systems/nft_systems.html

Parsons W. (2020, April 20). The 15 Best Fruits, Vegetables, and Herbs for Hydroponics. https://blog.1000bulbs.com/home/15-best-hydroponics-foods

Passive Sub-Irrigation. (n.d). DIY Hydroponics Blog. https://diyhydroponicsblog.wordpress.com/hydroponic-techniques/passive-sub-irrigation/

Static Solution Culture. (n.d). Hydroponic Vegetable Garden. http://www.hydroponicvegetablegardening.com/static-solution-culture/

Stephens, O. (2019, February 14). *A Brief History of Hydroponics.* The Hydroponics Planet. https://thehydroponicsplanet.com/a-brief-history-of-hydroponics/

Stephens, O. (2019, March 15). *How to Build a Deep Water Culture System.* The Hydroponics Planet. https://thehydroponicsplanet.com/how-to-build-a-deep-water-culture-system/

Stephens, O. (2020, January 5). *Indoor or Outdoor Hydroponics? How to Decide?* The Hydroponics Planet. https://thehydroponicsplanet.com/indoor-or-outdoor-hydroponics-how-to-decide/

Sub-Irrigation System. (2019, March 30). Maximum Yield https://www.maximumyield.com/definition/3495/sub-irrigation-system

Turner, B. (n.d). *How Hydroponics Works.* How Stuff Works. https://home.howstuffworks.com/lawn-garden/professional-landscaping/hydroponics1.htm

Valdez J. (2017, March 14). The Best Crops for Raft Systems (DWC). https://university.upstartfarmers.com/blog/best-crops-for-raft-systems

What Is a Passive Sub Irrigation System? (2013, January 10). Gator Hydroponics. http://gatorhydroponics.com/what-is-passive-sub-irrigation-system/

What Is the Nutrient Film Technique - NFT? How Does It Work? (2018, December 30). Green and Vibrant. https://www.greenandvibrant.com/nutrient-film-technique

Why Coco and Run to Waste. (n.d). Glandore Hydro. https://glandorehydro.com/article/why-coco-and-run-to-waste/

Wick Systems. (n.d). Home Hydro System. http://www.homehydrosystems.com/hydroponic-systems/wick-system_systems.html

Wick Systems. (n.d). Smart Garden Guide. https://smartgardenguide.com/what-is-wick-system-hydroponics/

Lastly…

If you enjoyed this book, then I'd like to ask you for a favor, would you be kind enough to

leave a review for this book on Amazon?

It'd be greatly appreciated & will likely help other avid green thumbs with their projects! I read EVERY review I receive and each one helps me to serve each and every one of you better, so your feedback is highly valued!

Thank you,

Basil Green

www.ingramcontent.com/pod-product-compliance
Lightning Source LLC
Chambersburg PA
CBHW081400070526
44583CB00020B/2618